About the Author

Michael Berg is the director of The Kabbalah Centre, as well as an author, scholar and teacher. Having been born into a kabbalistic tradition as the son of the Rav and Karen Berg, Michael steeped himself in the wisdom of the Zohar at a young age, and was the first person to translate the entire 23-volume Zohar and commentary from ancient Aramaic into English, beginning this monumental task when he was only 18 years old, and completing it ten years later.

Adept at combing through ancient materials and distilling complex information into elegant language, Michael has become a best-selling author with a worldwide following. His books include Becoming Like God, Well of Life, The Secret, The Way. He also edited Rav Ashlag's pillar works: The Wisdom of Truth, And You Shall Choose Life, On World Peace, The Thought of Creation, and The Light of Wisdom, as well as translated and edited Beloved of My Soul, Rav Brandwein's written correspondence to Rav Berg, a book presenting rare teachings through which the mantle of leadership of the Centre was transferred.

Michael currently lives in New York with his wife Monica and children, David, Miriam, Joshua, and Abigail, and lectures all around the world.

SECRETS OF THE BIBLE

Kabbalah Centre Publishing is a registered DBA of Kabbalah Centre International, Inc.

For further information:

The Kabbalah Centre
155 E. 48th St., New York, NY 10017
1062 S. Robertson Blvd., Los Angeles, CA 90035

1.800.Kabbalah www.kabbalah.com

Printed in Canada, February 2022

ISBN: 978-1-57189-769-5
ebook ISBN: 978-1-57189-818-0
Secrets of the Bible

Design: HL Design (Hyun Min Lee) www.hldesignco.com

SECRETS OF THE BIBLE

TEACHINGS FROM KABBALISTIC MASTERS

MICHAEL BERG

TABLE OF CONTENTS

LEVITICUS

NUMBERS

DEUTERONOMY

INTRODUCTION

History has been shaped by people like Abraham, Moses, and Rav Shimon —people for whom the surface of things was only the beginning of a quest for meaning. As my father, Rav Berg, eloquently puts it: "There have always been those who looked for the word within the word, the thought within the thought, the meaning within the meaning." That search for hidden significance lies at the heart of Kabbalah, the ancient wisdom that reveals and grants access to the spiritual forces that drive our material world.

We kabbalists believe that there are three miraculous sources for this knowledge of how the universe functions—and by miraculous, I mean actually imbued with spiritual power, with the Light of the Creator. One of these is the Torah, also known as the Five Books of Moses, or the Old Testament. The other two are the oral transmission of laws from the Creator to Moses on Mount Sinai, which are codified in the *Talmud* and the *Zohar*, the *Zohar* being the series of books authored by Rav Shimon bar Yochai, that decipher the Bible. Kabbalists believe that the stories in the Torah are not just meant to be understood on a literal level, but that, on a deeper level, they use analogies and code to reveal the spiritual underpinnings of everything we see and experience in the world today.

In this spirit of inquiry, I have drawn from the wisdom of the *Talmud*, of the *Zohar*, and of great kabbalists, scholars, and sages throughout history, for insights into the Five Books of Moses. As you will see in the pages ahead, I take special pleasure in moving off the beaten path to find fresh, unusual, and even surprising ways both to understand familiar stories like Noah's Ark or the parting of the Red Sea, as well as to offer new perspectives on more arcane portions like Chukat, with its detailed red-heifer purification ceremony. Taking advantage of the kabbalistic understanding that our soul transcends this lifetime, we will see how people long considered evil, like Korach, who rose up against Moses in the Book of Numbers, or Esau, who threatened to kill his brother, Jacob, are actually righteous souls, elevated spirits working on their correction, or *tikkun.*

Kabbalists believe that the Torah does not just contain secrets that we can use to transform our lives, but that the very letters and words of the Torah contain powers for good that we can unleash in our lives just by reading them. Indeed, on each Sabbath connected to a particular portion, the souls of the great spiritual giants we read about come back to this world to help us, teach us, and share their access to the Light of the Creator. So, for example, on the Shabbat of Chayei Sarah, the souls of Sarah and Rebecca give us direct access to the power of sharing and make the all-important distinction between sharing as a servant and sharing as a victim; on the Shabbat of Vayetze, we receive assistance from the souls of Jacob and Rachel in achieving true love; and on the Shabbat of Chukat, when Moses was accused of sexual betrayal, we tap into the consciousness that minimizes the ego, and with it, the power of death.

As we uncover the secrets of the Bible using the miraculous tools of the *Zohar*, the *Talmud*, and the *Midrash*, we don't just learn in the academic sense. Our awareness literally shifts as the hidden messages open conduits to the Light of the Creator and help us to acknowledge and accept our role as stewards of its boundless power. That difference will then express itself in every aspect of our everyday lives: In our families, in our friendships, in our jobs, in the way we love and the way we share. How could we not be affected? For as we open up to the hidden Light in the Torah, we drive away the shadows of our human frailties to reveal the endless beauty that is the essence of our souls.

It is my hope that these teachings awaken within you wisdom, inspiration, and Light.

Blessings,
Michael Berg

GENESIS

BERESHEET

On the morning of Beresheet some years ago, I just didn't feel like getting out of bed. Beresheet, which means "in the beginning," is the biblical portion read during the first Shabbat of the Torah reading cycle, a very important day. As I considered whether or not to make the trip to pray at The Kabbalah Centre, I found myself asking a larger question: Why do we attend services at all, whether they are at The Kabbalah Centre or at our synagogue or church? Why don't we just pray at home? Certainly one compelling reason is to see our friends and family, but we could create a weekly book club or poker game, which could just as easily fill that social need.

The *Zohar* tells us that each of the seven days of Creation in the Torah is referred to by a number—the second day, third day, fourth day, fifth day, etc.—with one exception. The Torah does not call the very first day of Creation *yom rishon*, or "first day," as we might expect, but rather *yom echad* (one day). The shift underscores that this is a singular day—a day of unity, a day to celebrate that we are one.

Kabbalists explain that when people gather together for services, the connections they make to the Torah and to each other have great value. But even more important is the gathering itself, an act that allows more Light to be revealed. And more powerful yet are those times when we gather together *in unity*. This is the special message of Beresheet conveyed by the words *yom echad*: one day. When we gather in unity on this first day of the year, we recreate the conditions that prevailed at the dawn of Creation. This moment, like that one, has the potential to reveal a phenomenal amount of Light.

The *Zohar* says that, unfortunately, most of us do not truly see. We may have eyes to navigate the physical realm—the world of our senses—but we are blind to the spiritual realm. If we only had the eyes to see it, we would be astonished by how much Light is generated when we come together in unity. We would never again have any doubt about the need to gather as one and to become attuned to each other as a single spiritual entity.

We know some of this intuitively. There is something magical that occurs when we gather for services on Shabbat. We all feel it. Yet things sometimes get in the way of that feeling, and one of them is routine. We all fall into repetitive patterns of behavior, some of which can be very helpful, like studying the Torah or attending Shabbat. But when our spiritual life starts to become routine, we lose the ability to achieve unity. Our minds are elsewhere. We are not fully engaged in *this* moment, listening to *these* words of the Torah. Beresheet provides us with a vitally important reminder that in this moment, everything is new. As the year begins with this first Shabbat, we stand together at the dawn of Creation, when all things are possible.

So *why* is the act of gathering so important? In speaking of Beresheet, the kabbalists say that giving others the ability to do their spiritual work is even more important than doing our own. Yes, we should think about this Shabbat as a time for making our own connections and revealing Light for ourselves and for our families. But even more valuable is the role we can play as a conduit, as a way of allowing everyone else to reveal *their* Light. Paradoxically, this dual consciousness—of desiring to make our own connection as well as wanting to serve others—is necessary in order for us to partake of the Light of the *echad*, the Light that is created by unity, by all of us joining together to participate as one.

On this, the first Shabbat of the year, we are reawakened to the power of community. Every one of us has our own spiritual work, but if we want to truly partake of the greater gift that is community, we have to give of ourselves in ways both great and small. Beresheet calls on us to renew our commitment to the people around us, knowing that the amount of Light we can reveal ourselves pales in comparison to the amount of Light we can reveal when we stand together.

As we will seek to do with all the biblical portions, we will consider what Beresheet tells us literally, and we also probe more deeply to find the inner Light that it sheds on the spiritual dimensions of the Creator's work. One of the many significant stories in Beresheet is the tale of Adam and Eve, the snake, and the Tree of Knowledge of Good and Evil, which begins with the Creator putting Adam and Eve in *Gan Eden*, the Garden of Eden. When the Creator places Adam and Eve in the Garden of Eden, He tells them that they may eat from all the trees of the Garden except one, *Etz haDa'at Tov veRa*, the Tree of Knowledge of Good and Evil. The snake then approaches Eve and tricks her into breaking the Creator's rule. When Eve gives the apple to Adam and he eats of it, they both fall spiritually, giving death the opening to enter our world.

In writing about Eve, the famous Moroccan Talmudist and Kabbalist, Rabbi Chaim ben Attar (also known as the *Or HaChaim*) asks, "How did this happen? How did Eve fall?" I find this question fascinating. The *Or HaChaim* tells us that Eve had no awareness of the existence of the negative force that some call Satan, or the Opponent, also known to kabbalists as the ego, or the Desire to Receive for the Self Alone. Eve came into this beautiful world with the understanding that it was all good: Adam was good, Eve was good, the animals were good, and the trees were good. When the Opponent came to her in the form of the snake, she had no idea that he was trying to trick her. If Eve had known the Opponent existed, of course she would have taken time to think through what his words meant and would have figured out that they made no sense. But she had no such knowledge.

This story in Beresheet awakens within us an appreciation of a basic lesson: There is an Opponent in this world, and we must be wary of him. If Eve had possessed that one piece of information, we all would not be here, struggling to bring more Light into a world full of suffering and death. The *Or HaChaim* also asks a question we have all put to ourselves at one time or other: If the Creator is never-ending Light, why did He allow the creation of the snake? The answer has to do with free will: The Creator wants us to make our own choices, to be virtuous because we choose to be and not because we have to. Now that we humans made the choice that led to the fall from Eden, the only way we can remove the pain, suffering, and death that entered the world is to overcome the Opponent who is making us doubt, who keeps misleading us. The snake—and the Opponent he represents—gives us the ability to grow spiritually, for without resistance there is no growth. Only in this way can we achieve *bila hamavet lanetzach*—the removal of pain, suffering, and death from our world.

There are two types of people in this world: There are "good" people, those who make some mistakes, but in general are kind and loving; and there are also those who have fallen, who have done real damage. Who is more important: A good person or someone who has fallen? The *Or HaChaim* tells us is that it is the fallen—those who have harmed others—who are more important to our world. Those who are born good and stay that way will not spiritually elevate us. But those for whom the Opponent is strong have a chance to bring about transformation. This is another reason why it is so essential to gather together in the spirit of unity, for in this way we can help each other—those who have fallen as well as those who have performed selfless acts of kindness. Now we can work as one to draw down more Divine Light.

As the *Or HaChaim* puts it, the Light that we receive is dependent on the difficulty of our work. If the Opponent were even one iota weaker, none of us would have a chance to contribute to the ultimate removal of pain and suffering from this world. Not only is the Opponent necessary, but his importance is magnified by his strength. For where is the most Light revealed? Where the opposition to the Light is greatest.

Any time we come together in prayer, we reveal Light. We gather on special occasions such as *Rosh Hashanah*, *Yom Kippur*, and *Sukkot*, and of course we generate Light on these happy occasions. But we can reveal more Light at times when the Opponent is strongest, when life is dark and difficult. It's more important than ever for me to go to synagogue on a day when I really don't feel like getting up and out of the house. Times like this are special opportunities to reveal Light.

In Beresheet, the Torah says: *In creating our world, the Creator saw the Light that it was good.* The *Midrash* explains that this first Light shone for thirty-six hours and then it was concealed, for the Creator feared that if the Light shone all the time, people might use its power for negative ends. As the great eighteenth century mystic, Rabbi Yisrael ben Eliezer, or the Baal Shem Tov, puts it: "Therefore, this Light was hidden. Where is that Concealed Light—which is called the *Or HaGanuz*, the Light that was too great to be left in our world—concealed? It was concealed in the Torah."

There are many stories where we learn that the kabbalists, including the Baal Shem Tov, had the ability—through their reading of the Torah and specifically, their reading of the *Zohar*—to see everything. Through our studies, each of us can attain this elevated spiritual level. What does this mean? The following story about one of the students of the Baal Shem Tov provides us with some answers.

Rav Baruch of Kaminka, a student of the Baal Shem Tov, was an ox trader at a time when many of the animals sent to market were stolen along the way. One day, Rav Baruch sent some of his oxen to market to be sold. As they disappeared around a bend in the road, Rav Baruch was overcome with concern that something might happen to them, so he sent his son, Rav Josef, to ask the Baal Shem Tov for advice. What could be done to keep his oxen safe?

The Baal Shem Tov told Rav Josef, "You should have come to me before your father sent your oxen to be sold, for then I could have ensured they would be protected." With that, the Baal Shem Tov opened the *Zohar* and began to read. After a few minutes, he said to Rav Josef, "I see that your oxen have not been stolen." Astonished, Rav Josef asked, "It says that in the *Zohar*?" to which the Baal Shem Tov replied, "With the Light that is called Concealed Light, you can see everything: Everything that was, everything that is, and everything that will be. If a person merits, through study, to connect to the *Or HaGanuz*, to the Concealed Light in the Torah, he or she will have the ability to see everything, everything in our world—the most spiritual *and* the most mundane." Then the Baal Shem Tov turned to Rav Josef and paused for a moment, as if to give his words special emphasis: "Did you think all I saw was the oxen?"

As the *Zohar* says, there are those who can see and there are those who cannot. But thanks to the gift of the *Zohar*, every single one of us has the *potential* to see everything—not only on the Shabbat of Beresheet, but every time we open the *Zohar*. There are endless levels to the *Zohar*, including physical, spiritual, and Supernal, and sometimes it will help us see into all of them just as clearly as the Baal Shem Tov did. This insight may come as an awakening of the heart so that the next time we have a decision to make, for instance, we will do so with a little bit more kindness and generosity of spirit.

In Rome, some of the more opulent bathhouses contained huge baths decorated with elaborate artwork. If the water in the bath was filthy, you could no longer see the beauty of the decorated tiles. However, once you removed the dirty water, the artwork stood revealed in all its glory. The *Midrash* explains that this describes Creation itself, a time when the world was completely in darkness. This darkness (*tohu vavohu*) was like dirty bathwater. Nothing new needed to happen for Creation to take place; all that was required was the removal of the darkness, or dirty water. *The process of Creation did not require something new. It required taking away the darkness so that the beauty of what was already there could be seen.*

This is also true of our world today. The *Midrash* says that if we repeat the phrase "*vayechulu hashamayin ve ha'aretz,*" or "the Heavens and the Earth became complete," we can reveal the perfection that underlies all things; we can become partners in the Creation of our world. Pain, suffering, and death are just illusions, dirty water that obscures our view. As Rabbi Israel of Koznitz puts it, there will come a time when we will look back and realize that this perfection was right here in front of us, all along. We just didn't see it.

Most of us believe that when we achieve our spiritual goals, something new will appear in our lives or things will somehow change. It's not going to happen. The *Midrash* explains that when pain, suffering, and death are finally removed forever, the result will not be something new. It will be like seeing beauty where it was all along, or like looking all over the house for our glasses or our keys, only to come back to our desk to see that they were sitting right there all the time.

The *Midrash* says that this change will occur in an instant. How can this be when there is still so much work to do in our world? Because perfection is already here. Don't be fooled by the filthy water covering the hand-painted tiles. Just drain it. No matter what happens in our lives, no matter what someone does to us, no matter what we think of ourselves, perfection underlies it all. If we think that we have to create something new, we will never get there. We have to realize that perfection exists now. *We are perfect. The perfection of the world is here now.* Our work is simply to remove the illusion that tells us otherwise. And the best way to do it is together. As one.

NOAH

It always gives me special pleasure to share insights from the *Zohar* that are not commonly read or considered. After the *Zohar* was first printed, sections were later found and included, and these became known as the *Hashmatot haZohar*, the missing *Zohar*. This is where I came across a reference to the story of Noah that struck me as both important and beautiful.

When Noah first came out of the ark after the flood and witnessed the destruction of the world, he broke down and wept. In his terrible pain, Noah called upon the Creator, saying, "You have been called merciful. You should have had mercy upon Your creatures." Despite Noah's obvious distress, the Creator showed little sympathy. Instead He said to Noah, "*Now* you are crying? Noah, I came to you before the flood to awaken in you the desire to beg for the world. When I told you I would bring destruction upon the world and instructed you to make the ark, *that* is when you should have wept and prayed and begged for mercy for the world. Yet you did not."

In the *Zohar*, the great sage Rabbi Yochanan says there is a difference between Noah and the righteous people who came after him. Unlike Abraham, Noah did not do his utmost to protect people from the wrath of the Creator. When the Creator told Abraham that the people of Sodom and Gomorrah were doing terrible things, Abraham immediately begged the Creator to spare them. He asked the Creator, "If there are forty righteous people in these cities, will You avert their destruction?" Abraham continued to beg that the cities be spared until he had negotiated the number of righteous people required down to only ten; at that point, he said to the Creator, "Then save the towns for them." The *Zohar* tells us that Abraham stopped at ten because he was so confident that there were ten righteous people in Sodom and Gomorrah that he assumed his plea had been successful.

After the Israelites sinned by making the golden calf and the Creator said to Moses, "Let me destroy them," Moses immediately began praying. Like Abraham, he was unrelenting in defense of his people. According to the *Zohar*, Moses pleaded with the Creator, "Take my life here in this world. Take my life in the World to Come. Blot me out of Your Book. Leave me with nothing, but save them." The *Zohar* tells us that the Israelites would have been destroyed, had not Moses, the Creator's chosen one, refused to allow this judgment of his people to result in their destruction.

We have here three examples: Abraham, who negotiated forcefully to save Sodom and Gomorrah until he believed he was successful; Moses, who begged to save the Israelites and succeeded in staying the Creator; and Noah, who did not pray, negotiate, or beg. As the *Zohar* puts it: "He built the ark, and the whole world perished."

So why did Noah not pray? We know he was a righteous person or he would not have been chosen by the Creator to build the ark, populate it, and survive the flood. Was Noah somehow indifferent to the fate of others? Or did he believe that his virtue placed him above the rest? To help explore these questions, let me offer a story by way of analogy.

A person with poor credit approaches a wealthy man to ask for a loan. Even though the wealthy man knows this supplicant has bad credit, he agrees to lend him the money. Then another borrower comes along who has an even worse credit history than the first. While the wealthy man is considering this second loan, the first borrower stops by and pleads tirelessly on behalf of the second man. This may be kind, but is it wise? At risk is not only that the wealthy man will refuse the second borrower, but that he will change his mind about the first loan, having lost confidence in that borrower.

This was Noah's concern. Noah believed he was skating on thin ice. The Creator had promised to save him, but Noah didn't want to draw too much attention to himself by begging on behalf of others, for fear that the Creator might have second thoughts about sparing Noah, his family, and all the denizens of the ark. The *Midrash* suggests that on one level, Noah was not mistaken: He needed the purification of the flood almost as much as the rest of his generation, but because he was fortunate enough to be enclosed in the ark that the Creator had asked him to build, Noah was protected from death and destruction.

We have been comparing the decisions of Noah, Abraham, and Moses, yet in many ways, this comparison is not fair. Abraham was a very righteous person, and Moses was one of the highest souls that ever came to this world. Simply put, Noah was not on their level of righteousness. Nevertheless, as the great sage Rabbi Elazar says in the *Zohar*: "It was from Noah's piety that he believed that he should not ask." It was not that Noah did not care, but that he believed he did not deserve to make a request of the Creator.

The *Zohar* offers us a crucial insight that can prevent us from making the same mistake as Noah. Rabbi Elazar says that Noah should have asked the Creator for mercy for the world. Not only might the Creator have been receptive to an appeal, but He would have been pleased that someone would defend, and speak well of, His children.

How do we know this to be true? In the Book of Judges, we find that God chose Gideon, a young man from an otherwise unremarkable clan of the tribe of Manasseh, to free the people of Israel and to condemn their worship of idols. Gideon was not especially righteous, nor were his parents. So why was Gideon chosen? It was not because of his connection to the Light of the Creator, nor because of his strength or wisdom. It was because Gideon "spoke well of Yisrael," because he asked for good things for the Israelites that the Creator said to him, "You will have all the power, all the Light you need to save them."

Noah did not understand that even if we have no Light, no special claim to virtue, or even if we are evil, as long as we have a true desire to help another person, that desire will connect us to the Creator. And the Creator will give us everything we need to provide that help. When most of us have an impulse to make a difference, we question our ability to do so. And with good reason. The fact is that most of us do not have enough wisdom or Light or virtue to give us confidence. Yet from the example of Gideon, we learn that we don't need any special qualities or gifts. All we need is a pure desire to help.

The Creator told Noah that he had missed a great opportunity. Noah's mistake lay in believing that this was a matter of his own level of righteousness—whether or not he had merit enough to ask that the world be saved. If Noah had simply asked for mercy out of a true desire to help, that one desire would have granted him access to everything he needed to save the world.

So what does this mean when it comes to the way you and I interact with other people? What does it mean for our work in this world? When someone in our life needs help—even someone we may have met only recently—we may well have the wisdom or wealth or personal connections to assist this person. And although these resources can be useful, there is a far more powerful—and effective—way to help them. We know that speaking ill of people can cause terrible damage, but the inverse is also true. Speaking well of someone out of a genuine desire to have good things befall him or her gives us the power to save the world. This is what the Creator was saying to Noah. Like Gideon, Noah could have spoken well of others, truly desiring the best for them. And perhaps, like Moses, he could have saved them.

The *Midrash* explains that at the very moment that Abraham said to the Creator, "I want goodness, not judgment, to come down to this world," he rose to his extraordinary spiritual height. According to the *Midrash*, the Creator responded to Abraham's request by saying, "There have been ten generations from Noah until you, Abraham. Of all those who lived in those generations, I want to talk only to you. I have no desire to be connected to or to talk to anybody else. You, Abraham, are chosen above everyone who ever lived until this time." Abraham was anointed and set above all other righteous people because of his pure desire for the common good.

You and I can do this, too. You and I can save a person. You and I can save the world. We can do so by acting like Gideon and Abraham, by finding ways to awaken in ourselves a stronger and stronger desire to help others, knowing that it will be this desire alone—not our wisdom or wealth or spiritual connection—that will make the difference.

Noah's mistake was that once he realized that the flood was imminent, he thought there was nothing more he could do. So one thing we can learn from the story of Noah is that we should never accept anything as final. This requires a shift in consciousness that may be difficult for many of us, especially if we have been raised to believe that being cooperative is the same as being good. But this is a change that we need to encourage. A beautiful story from the first book of the *Talmud* illustrates this idea.

King Hezekiah was very ill when Isaiah the Prophet came to him and said, "The Creator has asked me to come to you and tell you to put your affairs in order. You are going to die; you will not live." At first, it seems as if the Creator is simply preparing the king for the end of his days. But what does "You are going to die; you will not live" mean? Why the redundancy? The Creator sent Isaiah to King Hezekiah to deliver a double message: That his life in this world is nearly over, and that he will have nothing in the next world either.

Understandably, the king was shaken by this news. He asked Isaiah, "Why is this happening to me?" Now at this point in King Hezekiah's life, he did not have children. Some people cannot have children, but in King Hezekiah's case, he had never tried. The sages of the *Talmud* tell us that the Light of the Creator was punishing King Hezekiah, not because he had no children, but because he was not even *trying* to have children.

When Isaiah pointed this out, King Hezekiah explained that his powers of Divine Inspiration had foreseen that if he had chosen to have children, they would have been evil. "I would rather not have children than bring more evil into this world," the king said. Isaiah the Prophet responded, "Why are you worrying about Divine matters?"

By posing this question, Isaiah was not questioning the prophetic power of Divine Inspiration or the specific prediction about the king's children. Isaiah the Prophet was telling King Hezekiah that it was not his job to worry about the future because things can change. Isaiah said to the king, "You must take care of your plans. Supernal matters are not for you to meddle with."

Upset with Isaiah, King Hezekiah did not address him by name, saying instead, "Son of Amoz, it is time for you to leave. This teaching I received from my great-grandfather: Even when the sword is already at our throat, we should not stop asking for mercy from the Creator. Even at that moment—just before our lifeblood is spilled—we should know that we do not have to die, that everyone can change their destiny."

After Isaiah left the royal chambers, King Hezekiah prayed to the Creator. And even before Isaiah had made his way out of the king's palace, the Creator came to him and asked him to return to King Hezekiah with the news that the Creator had heard the king's prayers. Not only would the king be healed of his illness, he would be granted fifteen more years of life.

So what lesson can we take from this story? The Creator sent Isaiah to inform King Hezekiah that he was going to die, but the king refused to accept that judgment. Like Moses and Abraham, King

Hezekiah did not acquiesce when he heard the Creator's message. Through King Hezekiah, we can see Noah's mistake more clearly, the better to profit from it. When the Creator came to Noah and said, "The only hope for humanity is that you survive My flood and have children," Noah took the Creator at His word and accepted His judgment. Instead of making Noah's mistake, we must never accept a judgment or decree, no matter how elevated its source or how weighty, for even the Creator can be persuaded to reconsider His rulings!

Through his error in judgment, Noah has provided us all with precious understanding. And every year on this Shabbat, when we read the story of Noah, we are reminded that we can change this consciousness of compliance. The conviction that nothing is ever final, ever, has always been a driving force in the life of my father, the Rav. I have done my best to learn from his example, and I share this wisdom from the *Zohar*, the Torah, and the *Mishnah* in the hope that your life, too, will be blessed by this insight. If God sends His prophet to you and the prophet says you are to die, do not accept it. If God comes to you and says the world is going to end, do not accept it. Nothing is final. You always have the power to tip the scales of fate.

LECH LECHA

When the Creator asked Abraham to set out for the land of Canaan, the Creator said to Abraham, "*Lech lecha,*" "You go." In those days, it was no small thing to ask someone to uproot himself and his family and travel a great distance. Not only was travel an arduous and expensive proposition, but it was dangerous. Great preparation was required. "You go" implies the tireless effort needed to fulfill the Creator's request.

The great kabbalists tell us that those who are connected to the Light of the Creator possess this quality of constant striving. We can see signs of this in the Creator's regard for Abraham. The *Midrash* says the Creator called Abraham *Yedidi,* "My best friend," and *Avraham Ohavi,* "Abraham, My beloved." The Creator connected to Abraham so strongly because He knew that Abraham would strive to accomplish whatever task he took on, regardless of its difficulty.

And there was no shortage of difficulties. From the very beginning of his journey to Canaan, Abraham ran into trouble. He went down to Egypt, where there was a famine in the land, and if this wasn't bad enough, when Abraham entered Egypt, his wife Sarah was taken from him and delivered to the Pharaoh so that he might enjoy the pleasure of her beauty.

In describing all the obstacles that Abraham faced, the *Midrash* uses the metaphor of Abraham running against river rapids with a herd of wild horses chasing him. This is a good way to view our own spiritual work. To be like Abraham is to ask ourselves, "Am I throwing myself into the rushing river? Am I willing to continue on and on as the raging waters thrash against me?"

Most of us are nowhere near this level of consciousness. Every so often, we will do something to push ourselves, but most of us would be overwhelmed by just the thought of living like Abraham. How could we possibly be strong enough to face famine or to have our spouse forcibly taken from us to serve at the pleasure of another? We couldn't do it. Fortunately, each Shabbat—but most specifically on the Shabbat of Lech Lecha—we have an opportunity to pray for the ability to strive tirelessly against all obstacles, for the fortitude that Abraham embodies. First, we must want it, and then *we need to ask for it.* Like Noah, if we don't ask for it, it will not come to pass.

Abraham changes the way we think about our spiritual work. Most of us see the goal of spiritual life as an easy, endless connection to the Creator. This, however, was not what Abraham sought. Abraham sought to fulfill his purpose knowing there would be nothing easy about it. Abraham knew that we come into this world to work hard. In *Ten Luminous Emanations,* Rav Ashlag reinforces this insight with his discussion of *bameitim chofshi*, the idea that the only time we are free from struggle is when we are dead.

Many great people throughout history have had angels appear in order to help or teach them. However, when angels approached the Gaon of Vilna, Rabbi Eliyahu ben Shlomo Zalman, he replied, "I do not want your help. I want to work for this wisdom." If an angel came to teach us, how many of us would turn that angel away? How many of us could even imagine such a thing? This sense of enthusiasm for the struggle permeates the Shabbat of Lech Lecha.

There were very few souls—in fact, Moses may be the only one—who came close to the level of joy that Abraham felt every day. According to the *Midrash*, even when Abraham was faced with famine in Egypt, he "was not angry and did not complain." Abraham was *excited* to wake up each day and push himself. This consciousness filled him with the Light of the Creator. No greater fulfillment can come to us than this.

The portion of Lech Lecha helps us to understand that we have been mistaken about what we should desire for our lives. We must ask not for a life of ease, but for the ability to strive tirelessly against obstacles and for opportunities to do so. To run against the current doesn't have to be discouraging. It can be invigorating and exhilarating and inspiring. This is the gift of Abraham on the Shabbat of Lech Lecha.

VAYERA

In the biblical portion of Vayera, we find that after the destruction of the cities of Sodom and Gomorrah, the daughters of Abraham's nephew, Lot, lay with their father and conceived children by him. The explanation given for violating the taboo against incest is that Lot's daughters believed that they and their father were the only remaining survivors in the world. The *Midrash* tells us that Lot's daughters said, "We will make alive, from our father, a continuation, a *zerah.*"

Why did Lot's daughters use the word *zerah,* or "seed," rather than the word "child"? They did so to indicate that their motivation for lying with their father was not principally to bear a child, but to accomplish something far greater: To plant a seed for the future. This seed represents the future manifestation of *Mashiach,* the Messiah, the revelation of the Light of *bila hamavet lanetzach,* of victory over death, and *Techiyat haMetim,* the Resurrection of the Dead.

It is significant that the seed of *Mashiach* is not being sown under more elevated circumstances or planted by a great soul or a person of royal blood. *Mashiach* will come from the spiritual lineage of a daughter who slept with her father to conceive a child. Why is the seed of *Mashiach* manifesting from such rough soil?

Rabbi Aharon of Karlin, who was revered for his piety and mystical gifts, explains that after Adam sinned by taking a bite of the forbidden fruit, the Supernal Lights, or sparks of Divine Light, fell into the depths of the *klipot*, the negative shells that engulf the Light here on Earth. From that moment, when our world was plunged into the depths of spiritual darkness, until the time when *Mashiach* will reveal himself again in our world, the purpose of humanity's spiritual work is to cleanse, purify, and elevate these sparks of Light. Since the revelation of the *Gemar HaTikkun*, the Final Redemption, depends on raising these sparks from the lowest levels of the *klipot*, the seed for the soul of *Mashiach* in this world has to come from the lowest relationship possible.

Rav Ashlag, founder of The Kabbalah Centre and one of the greatest kabbalists of the twentieth century, asks why the coming of *Mashiach* will take place in our generation. How is it possible that we can accomplish what great souls like Abraham, Moses, and Rav Shimon bar Yochai could not? Paradoxically, the fact that most of us have fallen low enough spiritually to keep company with the daughters of Lot serves the larger body of humankind well: For only from the depths of the lives we lead can we fully elevate those Divine sparks and bring that *zerah*, that seed, to manifest *Mashiach*. Abraham could not, nor could Moses or Rav Shimon, for their souls were too elevated. But we can.

The sages teach that *Mashiach* can only come in a generation that is either entirely pure or entirely negative. Our generation, plagued by war, corruption, and the ebb tide of spirituality, is as lowly as any. Yet because of this, we have the unique ability to elevate the original sparks of Divine Light.

The *Talmud* refers to a conversation between a great soul and the soul of a king who had reigned during a time when idol worship was rampant in the world. This great soul asked the king, "How were you able to worship idols?" The king replied, "If you had been alive at that time, you would have been the first in line. Idol worship is like any other desire, and we all have lowly desires that we act upon." Eventually, the *Talmud* tell us, those souls living at the time when idol worship was prevalent came together and asked the Creator to remove this intense desire from our world. Only when the Creator saw that one idol worshiper had succeeded in giving up this practice did He remove the seductive power the idols had over people. Only when someone has failed at something can he or she transform that energy.

In this case, one person made all the difference. The same principle holds true today, only the numbers have changed a little. According to the sages of Kabbalah, 320 sparks of Divine Light must be elevated in our generation, but even before that, when we achieve the elevation of 288 sparks, everything will change. In this context, I was once asked, "Why did Rav Ashlag leave this world? Why did he not choose to stay here?" It's a good question, for it makes sense that any true kabbalist, knowing that the time of the coming of *Mashiach* was drawing near, would wish to spearhead the movement toward *bila hamavet lanetzach*, or immortality. It's possible that Rav Ashlag realized that his generation was not going to achieve the removal of death, so instead, he did all he could to prepare the world: He wrote books, he taught Rav Brandwein, and he laid down many spiritual seeds. It's also possible that Rav Ashlag knew that he was not the one to bring *Mashiach*. Rav Ashlag was too elevated. It would take the people of our generation to bring the Messiah.

This knowledge that our generation has fallen to the lowest spiritual depths could be very discouraging if we did not see this as meeting a requirement for the ultimate triumph of immortality. Certainly the Opponent, also known as Satan, wants us to dwell on how low we are. So the next time you fall spiritually, the next time you look at yourself and think, "I can't possibly help another person; I can't possibly reveal any Light," remind yourself that we can reveal this Light precisely because we *are* so low. This insight is the powerful weapon that Vayera gives us, the tool with which to overcome the trickery of the Opponent.

Another inspiring spiritual lesson from Vayera comes to us through the story of the *Akedah*, the Binding of Isaac. Most of us inject a large element of selfishness, of the Desire to Receive for the Self Alone, into our relationships, even with the people we love most. No matter how pure our love is for another person, if there is selfishness attached to that love, the relationship is fated to end. Unfortunately for many people, it ends at death. There is a way, however, to make love eternal. The Creator explained to Abraham that by giving up Isaac completely, by being ready to accept the death of his son, Abraham earned the right to have his love go on forever.

When most of us are told to give something up, it's easy to convince ourselves that we have done it. We may cut back on our everyday spending, for example, to save money for a worthy cause, but inevitably we will return to our usual ways, only hoping that in the interim we have done some good. Abraham, however, had elevated himself to such a high spiritual level that when he decided, "I am giving up Isaac. I am willing to let him die; I'm willing to let him go," his thought was so pure that it manifested as a completed action. Therefore, there was no need for Isaac to die physically. The death of his son, Isaac, had already occurred in Abraham's mind, so he gained the benefit of the spiritual process he had to undergo.

This is the only way we, too, can hold on to the people we love, but for most of us, detaching from all selfishness in a relationship is extremely difficult. On the Shabbat of Vayera, we can pray for Abraham to help us in this task with the Light that he revealed at the Binding of Isaac, Light that shines throughout all of history. When we truly understand this and ask for Abraham's assistance, we can slowly but surely let go of all those people and things we are attached to in a selfish, egotistical way. The end result will be that nothing—and no one—has to die. We will have achieved *bila hamavet lanetzach*, the "removal of death forever." This is our spiritual work—the work Abraham began, and the work we now have to complete.

CHAYEI SARAH

In the previous portion of Vayera, we learned about the Binding of Isaac. The *Midrash* tells us that Abraham did not tell Sarah that he was going to sacrifice Isaac. Instead, Satan, the Opponent, told Sarah, and when she learned that Abraham was about to kill their son, Sarah died of grief. But Sarah's alleged reaction does not make sense. Someone on Sarah's spiritual level would not have greeted the news of Isaac's impending death with such a terrible response. She would have understood that something beyond the physical event was taking place, something of great spiritual significance.

This tells us not to interpret the story in the *Midrash* in a literal way. In fact, the great Kabbalist Rabbi Avraham Yehoshua Heshil, the *Ohev Yisrael*, also known as the Apta Rebbe, tells us that Sarah knew Isaac was *not* going to die. Beyond this, she knew that a tremendous Light was about to be revealed at Mount Moriah, the site where the Temple would eventually be built, and Sarah wanted to be a part of that great revelation of Light. But she had a problem. The Binding of

Isaac was going to take place imminently, and even if she rode a donkey, she would not reach Mount Moriah in time. So Sarah made a decision, right then and there. She chose to leave this physical world so that her soul could travel swiftly to Mount Moriah where the *Akedah*, or Binding of Isaac, was taking place.

There is a reason why the Bible says that Sarah died in Kiryat Arba, which literally means the Town of the Four. She died with a complete connection to the Name of God—the Tetragrammaton (*Yud, Hei, Vav*, and *Hei*), and Adonai (*Alef, Dalet, Nun*, and *Yud*). Sarah achieved this total connection by relinquishing all selfish attachments in her relationships with other people. She freed herself of the Desire to Receive for the Self Alone.

Sarah is the only matriarch whose death, funeral, and burial-place spark the kind of lengthy discussion we see in Chayei Sarah, underscoring her spiritual significance. But this biblical portion also goes on at considerable length to describe the process by which Isaac's wife, Rebecca, was selected. The man who conducted that process on behalf of Abraham was his closest and most brilliant student; according to the *Midrash*, his name was Dammeseq Eliezer, which means Eliezer from Damascus. Not only was Eliezer able to understand the wisdom of Abraham, he was also capable of conveying it to other people. Many students throughout history have had this ability: Rav Chaim Vital filled this role with Rav Isaac Luria, and Rav Abba did the same with Rav Shimon bar Yochai, to name just two. But in the case of Eliezer, we are talking about someone who attained a level of wisdom far beyond what we can imagine today.

The Bible says that Eliezer travelled to the city of Nahor, where Rebecca lived, and asked the Creator to give him a sign to identify a future wife for Abraham's son, Isaac. Not only does the Bible devote many words to this story, but it repeats them when Eliezer recounts the event in detail for Rebecca's family. Since we know that the Torah is very intentional in its use of language, that there are no extra or insignificant words, the *Midrash* asks why the Torah devotes so much attention to this story. In answer to this question, the *Midrash* says: "Greater are the words of the stories of the servants of the patriarchs than is the study of their children."

When Eliezer came to Nahor to find a wife for Isaac, he brought with him great wealth—animals, gold, and jewelry—but when Eliezer introduced himself to Rebecca and her family, he did so saying only, "*Eved Avraham anochi*" "I am the servant of Abraham." Eliezer could have introduced himself as Abraham's closest friend or as his most promising student, which would have been equally true. But Eliezer chose to describe himself as *eved Avraham*, the servant of Abraham.

As we know, the purpose of life is to transform our Desire to Receive to the Desire to Share. We can share by helping another person, or we can share at an even higher spiritual level by sharing as a servant. When the Torah describes the great heights that Moses achieved spiritually, the words used are *Moshe Avdi*, or "Moses, My servant." When we no longer feel that we have a choice about whether to give or not to give, our consciousness becomes that of a servant, not in the sense of lowering ourselves, but in the sense of elevating ourselves spiritually.

As we strive to understand how this works in everyday life, we need to differentiate between being a servant and being a victim. There are many people who give to their children, their spouse, or their friends because they feel obligated to do so, even when they don't really want to. These are victims of sharing. But those like Moses and Eliezer, who give with a whole heart, are servants of sharing. There is no need for them to be servants, yet they choose to take on that role. This is the way to the highest levels of the soul.

Recently, I had a lunch date with a friend who was wrestling with some personal issues. I was looking forward to our spending some time together and to possibly being helpful, but on the day that we were scheduled to meet, I had a long list of urgent matters to take care of. I was about to call my friend and postpone lunch when I remembered the concept of being a servant in sharing. I knew that if I truly wanted to grow this consciousness within me, I had to use it every day, which in this case meant making the effort to have this lunch anyway, regardless of feeling stressed.

During Eliezer's journey to find a wife for Isaac, he stopped at a well outside a distant village, where a number of women were gathered. Eliezer asked the Creator for a sign: Whichever woman replied to Eliezer's request for water by also volunteering to water all his camels would be the Creator's choice for Isaac's wife. If you or I were standing by a well and a man leading a caravan of camels came up and asked for a drink, would we even dream of offering water to his string of ten camels? It would be kind enough to give him a drink, but to water all his animals, too? Such an act goes beyond mere sharing; it becomes unreasonable sharing—or sharing like a servant. This quality was exactly what Eliezer was looking for.

The *Midrash* says that when Eliezer arrived at the well, a miracle occurred. The water from the well rose toward Rebecca so that she would not have to lower the bucket all the way down to the bottom. For most of us, such a miracle would be proof enough that the Creator had chosen this woman to be Isaac's wife. But Eliezer wanted certainty, and the only way to get it was to know if she was willing to be a servant in her sharing.

Most of us share, but how many of us share with the consciousness of a servant? I think if we are truly honest with ourselves, our answer would be almost never. It's unlikely that any of us will attain this elevated consciousness today or tomorrow, but by awakening a desire for it, we are taking an all-important first step. Like Eliezer and Rebecca in the portion of Chayei Sarah, we can achieve continuous growth in our connection to the Light of the Creator. We can achieve the elevated spirit of Sarah, who chose to leave her body when she wanted something more important: To attend the Binding of Isaac at Mount Moriah, where a great revelation of Light was taking place.

TOLDOT

Studying Kabbalah and the insights of the sages continually reminds us of the value of looking below the surface for meaning. When we do so, we may find that we have to revise our initial impressions of the meaning of a story in the Bible, for example. This is the case with the story of Toldot, and the complex relationship between Isaac and his sons, Jacob and Esau.

In the Torah portion of Toldot, Esau trades his birthright as first-born son to his brother, Jacob, in exchange for a portion of lentil soup. Later, after Jacob poses as Esau to trick their elderly, blind father into giving Jacob the blessing due the older son, Esau threatens to kill his brother. It's easy to read this story and see Esau purely as a villain. However, the Bible says: "Isaac loved Esau," which gives us a reason to look more deeply.

The lineage of Jacob and Esau began with their grandfather, Abraham, who was followed by their father, Isaac. According to the

Midrash as interpreted by Rav Mordechai Yosef Leiner, also known as *Mei HaShiloach*, when Esau spoke with his father, Isaac, he talked about lofty matters like the details of his spiritual work. Most people reading this *Midrash* think Esau was just a liar, that he wanted his father to *think* that he was a good man when, in fact, he was not. However, even if Esau had been the most cunning of liars, Isaac was too lofty a spirit to have been fooled by Esau's words.

Initially, Jacob and Esau started out in the same place: Both had parents who loved them; each was favored by one parent; and both were elevated in their spiritual work. There was one significant difference, however, Esau wanted his father not just to favor him, but to recognize how spiritual he was. This was why Esau flew into a jealous rage when he discovered that Isaac had given his blessings to Jacob.

Jacob's attitude was very different. The *Mei HaShiloach* tells us that Jacob separated himself from any need for his work to be acknowledged by his father; instead, he put his certainty in the Creator. He understood if he did the right thing, the Creator would make sure that the right thing would come to him.

Unfortunately, many of us can relate to Esau: We want recognition for what we do, and we're upset when we don't get it. The biblical portion of Toldot helps us understand just how powerfully this desire for recognition works against us. Our spiritual work must take place between us and the Creator. Ideally, we should keep those who are not directly involved from knowing too much about our spiritual life—especially our acts of sharing—for anonymous good deeds reveal the most Light.

The *Zohar* asks, "How could Isaac possibly not know the truth about Esau? Isaac had the *Shechinah* (the Light of the Creator) and *Ruach*

HaKodesh (Divine Inspiration) with him all the time." The *Zohar* explains that the true blessings that Esau and Jacob sought could not come from Isaac; they could come only from the Creator. Isaac was the conduit, but he could not give the blessings consciously, because if he had done so, he would have limited their power. The Creator arranged for a complicated scenario of deception and mistaken identity in order for the blessings to come to Jacob; concealed from Isaac's understanding, beyond his consciousness their power would be undiminished.

Kabbalist sages explain that the day of the blessings by Isaac was unique in the history of humankind because on that day, the Gates of Heaven were open to reveal to our world the entirety of the Light of Redemption. Isaac knew that this great Light of Redemption needed to be brought down into our world, but he also knew that Jacob could not handle it; despite Jacob's attention to his spiritual studies and his many other virtues, he was still not ready.

The revelation of Light in this world has three requirements. First, there is the Source—the Light in the Endless World—which is inaccessible to most of us. Secondly, we must have conduits to draw down this Light and to allow it to be properly received; Isaac drew down the Light of Redemption for Jacob, just as Rav Isaac Luria (the Ari), did for his student, Rav Chaim Vital. And lastly when the recipient, or Vessel, is ready to receive the Light, it can be made manifest.

When Isaac was getting ready to bless Esau, he told his son to prepare food for him. Rebecca overheard this, and knowing the Creator had chosen Jacob over Esau, she took Esau's clothes (the Vessel of Esau) and dressed Jacob in them. Rebecca explained to Jacob that on this day, there was to be a great revelation of the Light of the *Gemar*

HaTikkun, or Final Redemption. She also told Jacob that he was not ready to receive the Light. Having been so immersed in his studies, he had not yet experienced the pain that is in the world. To do this, he had to take upon himself the clothing of Esau.

Rebecca told Jacob then—and is telling us now—that to the degree that we take upon ourselves this burden of the pain in our world, we create the Vessel to receive the blessings of the Creator. There are tremendous amounts of Light and blessings we could be revealing, but we are not doing so today because of our unwillingness to take upon ourselves the clothing of Esau, the pain of this world.

On the Shabbat of Toldot, we can come to Isaac for blessings. He is here to give them to us, and with them the ability to help bring about the Final Redemption. But as the great kabbalist Rav Ashlag explains, we can only receive this tremendous infusion of Light once we have truly accepted the truth that lies beyond our studies. Only to the degree that we dress ourselves in the pain of this world can Isaac give us the blessings of the *Gemar HaTikkun.*

VAYETZE

Vayetze, which translates into "And he left," is the Torah portion that tells the story of Jacob's departure from the Holy Land after many years of living there with his parents. On his way north to work for his uncle in the town of Charan, Jacob spent the night at a place known as Beit El, or House of God. It was here that he had his famous dream of a ladder extending from Earth to Heaven, with angels ascending and descending it.

Who were these angels? The *Zohar* and the *Midrash* have many explanations. Rabbi Yonatan ben Uziel, also known as the *Amukah*, explains that the angels were sent to accompany Jacob after he left the house of his father, Isaac. According to the Bible, before the Creator destroyed the cities of Sodom and Gomorrah, He sent three angels to Abraham to warn him of the impending destruction. Two of the angels also decided to go to Sodom and warn its inhabitants that they had come to destroy the city. Because angels are not supposed to reveal Heavenly secrets, these two were banished from their places near the Creator. When the time came for Jacob to leave his home in Beer Sheva, the Creator gave the two angels an opportunity to redeem themselves by protecting Jacob, which they did.

Once the angels had safely escorted Jacob to Beit El, they were granted permission to re-enter Heaven, where they told the other angels about the remarkable man they had met and protected. These two angels showed the others how to descend the ladder between Heaven and Earth to see Jacob. The angels that Jacob saw in his dream ascending the ladder were the same two angels who had been granted permission to re-enter Heaven. Those descending were angels that desired to look upon the countenance of Jacob, having heard of his greatness.

The *Zohar* tells us that the Creator will not perform an important action without first informing either the prophets or the righteous people (*tzadikim*) on Earth. This is how righteous people come by the gift of prophecy, the purpose of which is to help create the most receptive environment possible for change in the world. It is my own belief that these two angels, who had overstepped their authority in Sodom and Gomorrah, helped to open up a channel so that Jacob could foresee the future. This was part of their spiritual *tikkun*, their correction.

Along with assistance from the two angels, Jacob's journey involved another astounding miracle. As we know, Jacob left Beer Sheva and traveled north through Jerusalem and Beit El to Charan. Beer Sheva is near the geographic center of present-day Israel, while Charan is all the way up north in southeastern Turkey. After finally reaching Charan, Jacob decided to travel right back to Jerusalem. On the way, he became tired and lay down to sleep in Beit El, and it was then that the Creator said, "Jacob is coming through My House; let Me ask him to stay the night."

The *Midrash* asks: "Why did the Creator reveal Himself to Jacob at Beit El as opposed to the city of Jerusalem, where the Light of the Creator rested at Mount Moriah, the place of the Holy Temple?" The *Midrash* explains that the part of Jerusalem on which the Holy Temple stands literally detached itself from the ground and traveled to Beit El to be with Jacob. The most important plot of land in the world traveled all the way to Beit El to be with Jacob!

But Jacob had passed through both Jerusalem and Beit El, the Creator's House, earlier in his journey. Why did the Creator not encourage Jacob to stop on his journey north and urge him to stay the night? The reason is that Jacob did not yet have the right consciousness. While Jacob was traveling north to Charan, he was worrying that Esau might try to kill him in revenge for his trickery in winning Isaac's blessing. Jacob also worried about spiritual matters, and with all these things on his mind, he did not think to stop and pray in Jerusalem as he traveled through the city. Once Jacob awakened himself in Charan, he realized his mistake and immediately decided to return to Jerusalem.

In Vayetze, we see that once a person decides to do the right thing—to do whatever it takes to connect to the Light of the Creator—miracles will occur to support that person. It was certainly not necessary for the Creator to detach part of Jerusalem and bring it to Beit El. But when the Creator saw that Jacob had awakened himself, had realized his mistake and would take unreasonable measures to correct it, the Creator sent miracles to assist him.

Seeing this, we ourselves awaken to an alarming implication of this biblical passage. When Jacob walked through Jerusalem without stopping, he received none of the Creator's blessings, support, or miracles. He did not receive the least little bit of assistance from the

Creator. Can you imagine how different history might have been if Jacob had not awakened himself in Charan? He would have carried on with all his spiritual work; he would have prayed all day and studied and done everything correctly. Then he would have asked the Creator, "Why are my actions not working? Why do I not feel Your assistance?" He would never have known that it was because he did not have the Creator in his consciousness while he traveled through Jerusalem.

One of the lessons of Vayetze is that we can perform many virtuous acts, but we receive nothing if we do not connect to the Creator. There are gifts, blessings, and even miracles destined to come our way, but we will travel right past the opening for them if we do not awaken. We can toil away at our spiritual work for our whole life without awakening ourselves, and if we do, we will never understand why we do not have the assistance of the Creator. On the other hand, it is a tremendous revelation to realize how many angels and how many miracles stand ready to attend our awakening. The Creator Himself is waiting.

One of the miracles that awaits us is the miracle of love. The Bible says that when Jacob arrived in Charan, he met Rachel and kissed her. This is one of those rare times in the Torah where we find an unmarried couple kissing. It is also the only time in the Torah where we catch a glimpse of true romantic love. Jacob is willing to come to his uncle, Laban, and say, "I will work for you for seven years so I can marry your daughter." When Laban agrees, Jacob is true to his word.

This may seem like a terribly long time to wait, but for most of us love is selfish; based on "What's in it for me?" This is not true love. To Jacob and Rachel, the seven years that they could not be together seemed to fly by in a matter of days, for their love was based on sharing. One of the gifts of Vayetze is that on this Shabbat, we can receive assistance to achieve true love. In its ultimate form, the love Jacob and Rachel achieved is known as the Desire to Share. Their love had nothing to do with what either one could get from the other. The love they shared was an appreciation of what they were both capable of giving. When he saw Rachel, Jacob viewed her as a chariot for *Malchut*. He recognized the Light that she could reveal for the world.

Jacob's love for Rachel was similar to the love many of us hope to have for the Creator. The *Zohar* says that such love is *yirat haromemut*, love based on appreciation. When we appreciate someone, in this case the Creator, this appreciation in and of itself awakens more of our love.

Many of us make a distinction between one kind of love and another—between the love that we try to awaken for the Light of the Creator and the love we have for our friends or our spouse or children. But at their purest, all of these forms of love are identical. On the Shabbat of Vayetze, we have a special opportunity to ask to become awakened. On this Shabbat, we can say to the Creator, "Please open our hearts; let us connect to You, and give us the ability to awaken true love."

VAYISHLACH

The Torah portion of Vayishlach opens with Jacob traveling to meet his brother, Esau, with whom he has not had any contact for many years. Knowing that Esau hates him for having stolen his birthright and his father's blessing, Jacob is understandably anxious about meeting his brother. The Bible tells us that prior to this meeting, Jacob prayed to the Creator, expressing his humility at all the goodness the Creator has given him. Keenly aware of his good fortune and prosperity, Jacob sends messengers ahead with gifts of goats, sheep, cattle, and asses for Esau. When he approaches Esau, he bows down seven times before his brother as an act of submission.

The Torah says that Jacob realized the only hope he had of protecting himself and his family was to be generous to his brother and to diminish himself. Only when Jacob saw Esau did Jacob realize what he was truly battling against. In that moment, Jacob knew that all of his spiritual work, all his prayers, all his study—none of these spiritual tools was going to help him, for his struggle was with his own ego. Jacob realized that his only hope was to lower himself.

It is written that the only way a person can become a *tzadik*, a righteous person, is to throw him- or herself down at least seven times (connecting to seven different spiritual levels). To understand this concept, we need to realize that most of us are like Jacob at the beginning of this story. We have our spiritual work, we have our prayers, and we have our study. We can prepare all we want for our battle against Esau, but all these tools will achieve nothing if we are ruled by the ego.

In order to subjugate the ego, first we have to truly appreciate the magnitude of our challenge. Metaphorically, the ego is as great as the forces of Edom that were arrayed against Jacob. Because most of us are still living like Jacob—proud of our possessions and our accomplishments—we need to understand that our only chance for victory is to diminish the ego's dominion over us. We cannot lie to ourselves about this. Nothing we once thought would save us from Esau—from the forces of darkness and of pain in this world—will assist us now. Humbling ourselves is our only effective choice.

In *Avodat Israel*, Rabbi Israel of Koshnitz explains that we can achieve the level of God and create miracles once we reach the spiritual level of *ayin*, or "nothingness," for here there is no ego. At the level of *ayin*, we neither care for nor worry about ourselves. Through true diminishment of our ego and annihilation of our own selfish desires, we connect completely to the Essence of the Light of the Creator; this gives us the ability to make miracles, provide blessings, and even grant redemption. Even when judgment is meant to come to a person, someone on the level of *ayin* has the ability to nullify this judgment and to change it into a blessing.

The *Zohar* says that once there are ten people in complete unity, *Mashiach* will come. What does this mean? It means that complete unity can only be attained when ten people have achieved the level of *ayin*, of nothingness. It means that if we want the Redeemer to appear, we can either strive to achieve a critical mass of people in the world who truly desire to share, whatever that number may be, or we can focus on ten people and get them to completely annihilate their egos.

If we can move one person one degree closer toward *ayin*, then the Light that goes forth is much more powerful than teaching a thousand people. This does not mean that we should strive to do the one thing and not the other, but it certainly means that we should move the goal of *ayin* toward the top of our list of priorities. If ten people achieve *ayin*, then *Mashiach* will come. Such is the power of nothingness.

Rabban Gamliel's tale in the *Talmud* provides us with further insight into *ayin*. "Once I was on a boat when we passed by the wreckage of another boat that had recently been dashed to pieces. I was worried because I knew some of the passengers on that boat. I knew Rabbi Akiva was among them. I thought that maybe, God forbid, Rabbi Akiva had died in that boat wreck. When I got off my boat, to my great relief I saw Rabbi Akiva teaching on the shore. I went over to him and asked, 'How did you survive the boat wreck?' Rabbi Akiva answered, 'I grabbed one of the planks of wood from the boat that was destroyed and floated on the ocean. Every time a huge wave came to take me under, I bent my head down.'"

Rabbi Yehuda Loew ben Bezalel, also known as the Maharal, tells us that the lesson of the tale is this: If a person diminishes himself, judgment cannot come to him. The spiritual logic is simple. If you are somebody, you can be judged; if you are nobody, you cannot. Rabbi Akiva understood this, so whenever the waves came to drown him, he ducked his head, or annihilated his ego. This is the same wisdom we see at work in Jacob's meeting with Esau. When Jacob saw the negative power of Esau coming toward him, he bowed down. When you are "not there," the forces of negativity cannot touch you.

When the two brothers did finally meet, Jacob introduced his family to Esau. He placed the handmaids, Bilhah and Zilpah, in the front with their children; and behind them, he placed Leah and her children; and at the rear, he put Rachel and Joseph. But where, the *Midrash* asks, was Dina, Jacob's only daughter? The *Midrash* explains that Jacob, fearful that if Esau saw Dina he would want to marry her, hid Dina in a chest.

The *Midrash* goes on to say that Jacob brought judgment on himself through this act of hiding his daughter. If Esau had seen Dina, there is a good possibility he would have married her, and by doing so, Esau might have become a better person. But because Jacob did not give Esau this opportunity to transform, terrible events transpired: Dina was later kidnapped and raped by Sechem's son.

Those of us who have children can identify with Jacob's dilemma. Esau was a negative person, so it's difficult not to feel that Jacob did the right thing. So why did such harsh judgment come to Jacob as a result? According to one explanation, Jacob was correct in hiding Dina in the chest, but he made a mistake as he did so. The words used to describe this mistake are: "He closed the lock too strong," which means that while the action may have been proper, the consciousness behind it was not.

Every so often, opportunities arise for us to help someone see his or her mistakes. The question we need to ask ourselves is whether we enjoy telling this person about his or her faults, or do we feel pain? Our action will be the same in both cases. We will tell them exactly the same thing in exactly the same way, but the difference comes in how we feel inside. Do we feel sympathy, or do we take pleasure in their discomfort? The person who truly loves others will feel their pain.

In the *Talmud*, there is a story about Rabbi Yehuda HaNassi and a calf that was to be slaughtered for food. Knowing it was about to be killed, the calf came crying and hid near Rabbi Yehuda. Rabbi Yehuda told the animal, "Go to be slaughtered; this is what you are created for." The *Talmud* then says, "Because Rabbi Yehuda did not have mercy on this animal, the Heavens decreed that judgment would come to him, and for thirteen years, Rabbi Yehuda suffered great pain."

Like Jacob trying to protect his daughter, Rabbi Yehuda was correct in what he said. Animals are in this world in part to provide us with a source of food; when they die, the sparks of Light within them are elevated. The issue was not whether or not his statement was accurate; it was whether or not he felt badly for the calf when he spoke to it. We learn from Rabbi Yehuda and from Jacob that we can do the right things, but if the consciousness behind our actions is not based on caring, then even a righteous act can lead to a harsh judgment. As we saw in Toldot, Jacob struggled with the ability to take on the pain of others, and as we now see in Vayishlach, this same limitation leads to suffering for both Jacob and his daughter.

In hiding Dina from Esau, Jacob made another error. He was not open to the possibility of redemption, the possibility that Esau might mend his evil ways. On this topic, there is a wonderful story about Rabbi Naftali of Ropshitz, who at one time was a student of Rabbi Mordechai of Neshchiz. Rabbi Naftali was very close to his teacher and spent all the holidays with him. One year, Rabbi Mordechai informed his student that he did not want to spend the coming Passover with him. Rabbi Naftali was hurt by this news and asked his teacher what he could do to change his mind, but Rabbi Mordechai did not answer him.

Rabbi Naftali wanted to spend Passover with his teacher so badly that he concocted a plan. He decided a few weeks before the holiday to make himself indispensable to the wife of Rabbi Mordechai. Rabbi Naftali worked hard to help her in the kitchen preparing the food for Passover, and sure enough, Rabbi Mordechai's wife was so grateful that she asked him to stay for the holiday meal. Rabbi Naftali replied, "Of course, I would love to, but your husband said that it would not be possible for me to spend Passover with you this year."

Just as Rabbi Naftali had foreseen, Rabbi Mordechai's wife went to her husband and begged him let to let Rabbi Naftali stay. Her husband finally conceded, saying, "If it is that important to you, I will let him join us, but I believe he is going to make tremendous trouble for me."

The morning before the Passover *Seder*, Rabbi Naftali began to feel the Light of Passover approaching. He went to the *mikveh*, the ritual bathhouse, and immersed himself in the waters, after which he went to the hall of study. While Rabbi Naftali studied, a man approached him in the hall and asked, "Can you show me where Rabbi Mordechai Neshchiz lives? I would like to speak to him before Passover."

Spiritually elevated people have a heightened sense of smell, and Rabbi Naftali detected that this man not only stank physically but spiritually as well. Rabbi Naftali responded, "How dare you ask to talk to my teacher before Passover? Do you know how elevated he is on this day? Now leave." And Rabbi Naftali practically threw the man out of the hall.

A few minutes later, Rabbi Mordechai entered and asked Rabbi Naftali if anybody else had come to study. Rabbi Naftali replied, "No, nobody significant has been here for a long time. I have been sitting alone." Rabbi Mordechai then asked him, "Has anybody at all been here in the past fifteen minutes?"

Rabbi Naftali replied, "There was a man, a filthy person who asked for you, but I told him that he could not waste your time and I asked him to leave." Rabbi Mordechai looked horrified and responded, "If you do not bring that person to me right now, you are never going to see me again."

Distressed by his teacher's outrage, Rabbi Naftali rushed out of the study and wandered all through the town, searching for the man he had dismissed, but he could not find him. As a last resort, Rabbi Naftali decided to search the local tavern. Sure enough, there was the man sitting at the bar, filthy drunk. Rabbi Naftali told him that Rabbi Mordechai wanted to see him.

The drunken man replied, "Do you know how much you embarrassed me? There is no way I will come with you." Rabbi Naftali began to plead. "If you do not come with me now to my teacher, I am finished. My teacher swore that I would never see his face again if I do not bring you to him now." With that, Rabbi Naftali picked up the drunken man, slung him over his shoulder, and carried him to his teacher.

During Passover prayers, this man—now bathed but still spiritually unclean—stood right next to Rabbi Mordechai. At the Passover *Seder*, again Rabbi Mordechai sat right next to this man, while Rabbi Naftali sat all the way at the other end of the table. During the entire meal, Rabbi Mordechai did not even say hello to Rabbi Naftali, and in fact, ignored him for the entire holiday.

Several weeks later, Rabbi Naftali approached his teacher to beg his forgiveness. Rabbi Mordechai said, "I want to tell you who this man is. Long ago, I had a very close student who had been with me for many years. However, at one point, he fell and continued falling until he was very low spiritually. It has been some fifteen years since then, and he has only gotten worse. Before this holiday of Passover, I had a vision of an awakening of purification within him and of him repenting. In the vision, my student said, 'I will go to my teacher one last time. If he takes me in, I will know that there is still hope for my soul. If he does not, I will know my life is over.'"

Rabbi Mordechai said to Rabbi Naftali, "I knew that if you were here with me during this Passover, you would mess up this opportunity of correction for this incredible soul. This is why I asked you not to attend. You were right in saying that this man was a filthy nobody, but this was his last chance to redeem himself. Had he not been given the opportunity to come to me before Passover, you would have had his soul on your conscience."

This story illustrates the point that even though we may recognize someone's negative nature, we must always be open to the potential for transformation. This was the mistake Jacob made when he hid his daughter from his brother, Esau. In addition to encouraging us to diminish our ego, the portion of Vayishlach reminds us to never lose sight of the possibility of redemption and that the potential for drawing Light grows only with the depth of our spiritual fall. We are awakened by the example of Jacob to appreciate the humility and care we must take when dealing with other people's souls.

VAYESHEV

Jacob had twelve sons and one daughter. The Bible says that Jacob loved Joseph, the second youngest son, more than the others, so much so that Jacob gave Joseph a beautiful "coat of many colors." Understandably, the other sons were jealous of Joseph. Adding to the tension, Joseph told his brothers of two dreams he had: One in which sheaves of grain that his brothers had gathered were bowing down to Joseph, and the other in which the sun, moon, and stars bowed down to him as well. The brothers took these dreams to mean that Joseph intended to rule over them, a prospect they did not relish. In fact, they were so resentful that they made a plan to kill him.

Yehuda, the fourth son, was effectively the leader of this group of brothers. He convinced the others not to murder Joseph, but instead to sell him to some passing Ishmaelites for twenty pieces of silver. Then the brothers dipped Joseph's coat in goat's blood and showed it to Jacob as evidence that Joseph had been killed by wild animals. Jacob mourned his son for many days and refused to be comforted.

Seeing his father's terrible suffering, Yehuda realized he had made a mistake. He stepped down from his leadership role with his brothers, married, and had children.

Rav Mordechai Yosef Leiner of Izbica, also known as the *Mei HaShiloach*, poses the question: "If Yehuda realized he had done something wrong, would he not want to work on himself spiritually?" If so, why did he get married immediately after he realized his mistake in encouraging the brothers to sell Joseph? The answer is that although Yehuda believed all hope was gone for his life, he thought his children could do some good in the world.

Yehuda named his first son Er, meaning "to awaken," in the hope that Er would awaken the Light of the Creator. Er, however, turned out not to be a good person. Yehuda's next son, Onan, was no better. The Creator made Yehuda understand in no uncertain terms that if he had no hope in himself, no spiritual life in his soul, he could have a hundred children and it was not going to make any difference. You cannot give to others what you yourself do not possess.

In the *Ten Luminous Emanations*, Rav Isaac Luria, also known as the Ari, explains that whatever Light comes down from the Creator to our world has to come through a channel or conduit, but if the person serving as a conduit does not believe that he or she has the ability to fulfill this role, then this person's children will also lack that ability. The *Mei HaShiloach* explains that only after Yehuda understood this could he father a son who was a positive force in the world. He named this son Shelah, which comes from the root word meaning "to let go." By this name, Yehuda implied that he understood he had made a mistake with his first two children.

While the level of trust we have in our ability to be a conduit for the Light of the Creator affects how much Light we can transfer to others, we must also be aware of falling prey to overconfidence. Yes, we are striving for complete certainty in our role, but we must avoid thinking that *our* own wisdom, *our* understanding, or *our* ability to share spiritual Light is the key. This, too, leads to darkness. The *Mei HaShiloach* tells us that the only way to bring the Redemption, the *Gemar HaTikkun*, closer to us is to acknowledge with a pure heart that we cannot accomplish this on our own; our certainty lies in the Creator.

In the *Midrash Rabba*, Rabbi Shmuel, the son of Nachman, describes Jacob's sons as busy with the sale of Joseph, Joseph as busy trying to survive, Yehuda as immersed in having children to achieve what he could not, Reuben caught up in his guilt, and Jacob lost in his grief. All these amazing spiritual channels were preoccupied. When we are caught up in our own feelings, we lose sight of the bigger picture, and lose awareness of the miraculous processes at work in our lives.

Joseph, Reuben, and even Jacob were absorbed in their spiritual work because they believed they could awaken the Redemption. Yehuda, on the other hand, realized there was nothing he could do on his own to correct himself, much less to bring about the *Gemar HaTikkun*. Instead, he cried to the Creator for help correcting his soul. In answer, the Creator told Yehuda that he, not Jacob or Joseph or any of the other brothers, but he, Yehuda, would be the one to plant the seed for *Mashiach*.

Once again, we have a paradox. Yehuda's understanding of powerlessness was the very quality that brought him close to the Creator. On the one hand, he gave up hope for himself, but on the other hand, he learned to put his hope in the Creator. He let the

Creator be the hand that guided him. And when he did, the Creator reached out to him.

Rav Ashlag says that when we do turn to the Creator, He gives us what we need—and no more. Imagine a homeless person approaching you and asking for money to buy a cashmere overcoat. Your natural reaction might be to laugh and keep walking. However, if the same homeless person approached you and said, "I'm hungry," you would be far more likely not to send him away empty-handed.

The Creator is the same way. If we come to the Creator and say, "I am doing a lot of spiritual work and I really think I am accomplishing a lot, but it would be nice if You could give me a little help," the Creator is likely to remain unmoved. But when we come to the Creator, knowing truly in our heart that there is nothing more we can do, and we say, "Please, I beg of You, correct my soul, bring the Redemption," this awakens the Creator's desire to help.

The Bible tells us that part of the reason why Joseph and his brothers did not get along was that Joseph's dreams seemed to imply that one day he would rule over his brothers. Another reason was that Joseph would tell his father, Jacob, all the things he saw his brothers do wrong. Rabbi Shlomo Hakohen of Radomsk, also known as the *Tiferet Shlomo*, says that we learn from this verse how dangerous it is to speak badly of another person. According to both the *Zohar* and the *Midrash*, when the Creator wanted to manifest our world, He asked the angels, "Should we create man or should we not?" There was a group of angels that said, "No, do not create man, for he is going to sin." Although these angels were on a very elevated level and correct in their prediction about humanity, they fell because they saw something wrong in humankind and gave words to it.

The angels who fell did not sin when they offered their opinion that humanity should not be created (angels have no free will and thus cannot sin), nor were they being punished by the Creator. They fell because of the working of a Universal Spiritual Law: If we look into darkness, we awaken darkness within ourselves.

Poison enters us when we see the bad in another person. My father, the Rav, says that according to medical science, genetic triggers for cancer lie dormant within most people, if not all of us. For reasons researchers don't yet understand, this disease awakens in some people and not in others. The *Tiferet Shlomo* explains that we unlock the dormant poison of death within us when we see the bad in others. Whether this is conscious or not makes no difference. Once we see the bad in someone, the poison is released.

The *Tiferet Shlomo* explains that the Creator embedded in all of us both physical and spiritual protections. Two things happen when we see darkness in another person. We awaken the dormant darkness within ourselves, and we remove the spiritual and physical protection from the Creator that keeps us from falling. Jacob saw with the eyes of Divine prophecy; he knew that Joseph was in great danger of being sold into Egypt as a slave, so he encouraged Joseph to go and see the perfection in his brothers. Unfortunately, Joseph did not obey his father, and many years of pain and suffering followed.

We see the positive aspect of this dynamic in Psalms 34:12: "Who is the man who desires life, who loves days, to see good...," the literal translation being: "He will live a long life to see goodness." If a long and happy life is what we desire, we have to concentrate on seeing the good in others. This is how we protect ourselves; this is how we keep those dormant forces of physical and spiritual darkness from ever being awakened; and this is how we keep the protection of the Light of the Creator.

MIKETZ

Vayeshev, the biblical portion before this one, ends with a tremendous amount of sadness. Jacob has lost his beloved son, Joseph, and is in mourning. Joseph's brothers are unsuccessful in lightening their father's burden of grief. After being sold into slavery in Egypt, Joseph is falsely accused of making sexual advances toward the wife of Potiphar, his master, and is sentenced to ten years in prison.

At the start of the portion of Miketz, Pharaoh has two disturbing dreams: One in which seven lean cows rise out of the river and devour seven fat cows, and one in which seven withered ears of grain devour seven fat ears. Pharaoh's wise men are unable to interpret his dreams, but his head wine steward, who had met Joseph in prison, remembers Joseph's extraordinary gift for doing so. Pharaoh orders Joseph pulled out of prison and brought before him.

Joseph interprets Pharaoh's dreams to mean that Egypt will face seven years of abundance followed by seven years of famine. He advises

Pharaoh to store surplus grain during the seven years of abundance. Impressed with Joseph's wisdom, Pharaoh has him released from prison and appoints Joseph his second-in-command, helping Pharaoh to rule over all of Egypt.

In the second year of the great famine, Jacob sends his older sons to Egypt to buy grain for the family. The brothers are brought before Joseph, but they do not recognize him. Knowing who they are, Joseph accuses them of being spies. The brothers plead that they are only buying grain and mention that they have a younger brother, Benjamin, awaiting them at home. Joseph demanded that they bring Benjamin to him as proof of their words.

Benjamin is brought to Egypt, but he, too, does not recognize Joseph. Joseph gives the brothers the grain they have come to Egypt to collect, but as the brothers prepare to leave, Joseph tells his steward to hide a silver goblet in Benjamin's bag. Then, after the brothers depart, Joseph sends his soldiers to arrest them for stealing the goblet.

When the brothers, including Benjamin, are dragged back to stand before Joseph, he tells them that Benjamin will have to remain a slave in Egypt as punishment for stealing Joseph's goblet. The brothers are in anguish, for now they have lost their younger brother, Benjamin, in addition to Joseph. What was Joseph's reason for creating this drama and for separating Benjamin from his brothers? Why did Joseph choose this particular pretext as a way of ultimately revealing his true identity to his brothers?

The kabbalists tell us that the twelve children of Jacob were not simply people; they were channels of the Light of the Creator. Each of them had his own spiritual task and his own role as a spiritual channel. Joseph's job was to gather all of the Light before it could be revealed in our world; he held the power that would unite the scattered Light and prepare it to be made manifest. When Joseph was first sold into slavery, all his brothers began to falter spiritually. They did not know why, thinking that the timing was just a coincidence. The reason was that Joseph was the force that held them all together and elevated them.

This illustrates an important lesson. When we are not aware of those people in our life who sustain us both physically and spiritually, we do not appreciate their assistance. It is only when those people are either taken away or step out of our life that we begin to realize how much we need them. The kabbalists say that when Joseph was separated from his brothers, Benjamin took his place spiritually. Although Benjamin was not on the level of Joseph, he still began bringing unity and spiritual elevation to the family, although once again, they did not attribute this growth to its proper source. Joseph realized that the only way to awaken their appreciation for Benjamin's assistance was to separate him from his brothers. This was the reason why the silver goblet was slipped into Benjamin's bag.

Joseph's plan worked to perfection. Once they were separated from Benjamin, the brothers did begin to appreciate his importance. This allowed them to begin the process of reunifying with both Benjamin and their long-lost brother, Joseph. Without this new appreciation, the brothers would not have achieved the level of unity required to reunite with their younger brothers.

Each one of us has people we appreciate in life, but there are others who assist us in physical and spiritual ways for whom we do not have enough appreciation—or perhaps no appreciation at all. If we do not awaken gratitude for them, our relationships with them will falter and break down. If we want to ensure their support, we have to awaken within ourselves a greater and greater appreciation for what they give us. Only if we are constantly growing in our appreciation can we be guaranteed to keep these important relationships healthy.

When Joseph was still in jail for his alleged sexual assault of Potiphar's wife, he interpreted the dream of Pharaoh's wine steward, who was in jail with him at the time. Joseph informed the wine steward that his dream meant that he would soon be released from jail and elevated to his previous post, once again serving at Pharaoh's side. When the wine steward was released, Joseph asked the man to remember him. The kabbalists ask, "Why did Joseph try to ingratiate himself with this other prisoner? Did Joseph not trust that the Light of the Creator would come and assist him to elevate out of his darkness?" In fact, Joseph spent two additional years in prison as a consequence of his lack of certainty in the Light of the Creator.

A great kabbalist, Rabbi David Shlomo Eibshitz, the *Arvei Nachal*, says that when two people achieve a level of friendship or love so complete that each puts the well-being of the other above his own, then the Creator will set aside all His other concerns in order to draw down Light upon these two people. As we act in this world, so we awaken acts from Above. The *Arvei Nachal* says that whenever we find ourselves in need of tremendous Light from Above, we should use this teaching. We should find a friend with whom we can bond in this way, and through an awakening of this kind of friendship, draw Light into our life.

However, it is important to understand that *both* parties in the relationship must feel truly selfless love to draw down Light from the Creator. Remember that Joseph's love for the wine steward was not reciprocated, and thus he remained in jail for two more years. But when we do invest our love in another person—and if that friend reciprocates with an equally selfless love—the Creator will set aside everything else to come and assist us.

The kabbalists draw our attention to the contrast between the terrible sadness at the end of the portion of Vayeshev and the tremendous joy that occurs at the beginning of the portion of Miketz. In so doing, they underscore the speed with which change can come. Genesis 41:14 describes how, after hearing that Joseph was a good interpreter of dreams, Pharaoh sent his soldiers to *vayaritzu umin habor*, or "quickly run" Joseph from the jail, so that he could prepare himself to see Pharaoh. This idea of "being run quickly" is an important one.

Often when we are in a difficult situation, we ask for assistance from the Creator, but we frequently make the mistake of thinking that the process is going to take time. We think that although the change we are looking for may come one day, there is still a lengthy process we must go through. But this is not the case. The Bible says *yeshuat haShem keref ayin*, "assistance from the Creator comes in a blink of an eye."

VAYIGASH

In 167 BCE, Jewish rebels (*Hashmonaim*) led by Judah Maccabee rose up against their Greek ruler, Antiochus, who had desecrated the Temple in Jerusalem. In a series of battles lasting some twenty-five years, the Maccabees defeated the much larger and better-trained Greek army. They reentered the Temple and purified it, after which one night's oil miraculously kept the Temple menorah lit for eight days, which would become the basis for our contemporary celebration of *Chanukah*. It is no coincidence that the story of Vayigash is generally read on the Shabbat after *Chanukah* because there is a link between the Maccabees who defeated the Greeks and the consciousness espoused by the biblical portion of Vayigash.

Vayigash begins with the words *Vayigash elav Yehuda*, or "Yehuda stood up to Joseph." This refers to Yehuda's resistance to Joseph's demand that Benjamin, their youngest brother, be a slave in Egypt. Yehuda protested that if Benjamin was forced to come to Egypt, their father, Jacob, would die of grief. What the kabbalists explain, and the

Zohar makes clear, is that like so many biblical portions, Vayigash is more than it appears to be—a story about events that took place thousands of years ago. Below the surface, it is describing the process of Redemption, which can come only when enough people "rise up," just as the Maccabees did with Antiochus and Yehuda did to the Egyptian lord he did not recognize as his own brother.

Vayigash elav Yehuda speaks of our elevation through what the sages call *azut dekedushah*, or "holy audacity." Rising up with holy audacity eventually led to the restoration of the Temple and the miracle of *Chanukah*. That a few thousand Maccabees were able to hold off and eventually defeat the powerful Greek army had nothing to do with military prowess; the miracle occurred because the Maccabees had *azut dekedusha* and *vayigash elav Yehud*a. They had the holy audacity to stand up to the Greeks.

In the previous biblical portion of Miketz, we saw Yehuda and his brothers brought low by Joseph and by the challenging events they faced. This, unfortunately, is our situation today: We are beaten down by the *Galut*, by the darkness in our world. The portion of Vayigash shows how we can change all that. Yehuda said to himself, "Even though we may not deserve to do so, we are going to rise up in this moment." The great gift of the Shabbat of Vayigash is that it awakens within us the strength to stand up for ourselves when we are being oppressed.

One of my students at The Kabbalah Centre runs a very successful business providing specialized services to companies large and small. This particular student is very down-to-earth. When I asked him what made his business special, he replied, "My clients receive nothing more from us than the strength to act on their own convictions. The good results then take care of themselves." This observation struck me as both astute and enlightened. Spiritual strength is a rare commodity in our world today. The courage and tenacity required to raise our hearts in our spiritual work is the hidden blessing of the Shabbat of Vayigash.

In the *Ta'anit* section of the *Talmud*, we find the story of Nakdimon ben Guryon, who some scholars believe is the same Nakdimon mentioned later in the New Testament. We know that during the *Shlosha Regalim* (the holidays of *Pesach*, *Shavuot*, and *Sukkot*), many people flock to Jerusalem from all over the world to celebrate these cosmic events. During one such time, many more people came to the city than were expected, taxing its resources until there was no water for them to drink.

Nakdimon ben Guryon, a wealthy man who lived in Jerusalem at that time, went to a Roman nobleman who owned wells of water and asked if he could use twelve of these wells to slake the thirst of all the Jews who had gathered in Jerusalem. Nakdimon ben Guryon promised that by a specified date, he would pay the Roman back with twelve wells filled with water, and if on that day Nadkimon was not able to do so, he would pay the man twelve pieces of silver, a king's ransom in those days.

Unfortunately, it was very dry that year. On the morning of the agreed-upon day, the nobleman sent Nakdimon a message, asking for the water or the money. Nakdimon replied calmly that the day was still young. That afternoon, Nakdimon received another request for repayment, to which he replied that there was time yet. Toward sunset, a third and more insistent message arrived: "Give me the water or pay me the money." Again, Nakdimon replied that the day was not yet at an end.

The Roman nobleman laughed when he heard this reply. It had not rained all year. Did Nakdimon really think that in the next few hours it would rain enough to fill twelve wells with water? So the nobleman went to the bathhouse, and Nakdimon went to the temple. Nakdimon covered his head with his *Talit*, his prayer shawl, and prayed to the Creator, "Master of the World, You know why I borrowed these twelve wells of water. It was not for me. It was not for my family. I did it so that all who came to this city to honor You should not suffer." Just as Nakdimon finished his prayer, the sky suddenly darkened with clouds and rain fell with such tremendous force that all the city's wells were soon overflowing.

The Roman exited the bathhouse at the same moment that Nakdimon left the temple. When they met in the street, Nakdimon jokingly said to the nobleman, "Now you will owe me silver, for I am giving you back more water than I borrowed."

The Roman answered, "I know that the only reason it just rained is because the Creator helped you. But it is still so overcast that we do not really know if the sun has already set. If I choose to say that it did, you will still have to pay me the money."

So Nakdimon went back into the temple, covered himself with his *Talit* once more, and again prayed to the Creator, "Master of the world, let the world know that You look upon us with favor, and that I am truly connected to You." Immediately the clouds disappeared, the sky cleared, and the sun shone brightly, still clearly above the horizon.

Here we have a story that contains two miracles. First, the Creator responds to Nakdimon's request for rain with a miraculous downpour. Then, in response to Nakdimon's second prayer, the skies clear and the sun shines. So which was the greater miracle? In the first instance, Nakdimon was running out of time. It was a great miracle, but it was born of desperation. The second miracle occurred when Nakdimon awakened his *azut dekedushah*, his holy audacity. He might have won his argument with the wealthy man over whether or not the sun had set, but instead he found within himself the courage and spiritual power to ask the Creator for another miracle—the second in as many hours! Thus the second miracle is more significant than the first.

When we are desperate, many of us may ask the Creator to assist us, but few among us have the holy audacity to say, "We are going to tell the Creator that He has to create this miracle." But *azut dekedushah*, holy audacity, is necessary to usher in the *Gemar HaTikkun*, the Final Redemption. It is a requirement both for the *Mashiach* consciousness needed to usher in the Messiah and for immortality, for *bila hamavet lanetzach* to come to this world. Knowing that we ask for miracles not for ourselves but for the world, we can be bold.

A beautiful section in the *Midrash* says that when the Creator created our world, He created the potential for the great Light that will end the darkness of this world. This is the Light that will be revealed in our world through what we call *Mashiach*, the end of the correction. This is the moment when humanity has reached the tipping point, when a majority of us has completed the work of removing the darkness and pain from our world.

At The Kabbalah Centre, when we study about immortality, which can also be described as the removal of suffering from our world forever, we find that this is a difficult concept for most of us to accept. Do you know who else has trouble with this? The *Midrash* says that the most negative angel, the Satan, also does not believe that immortality is possible.

When the Satan said in effect to the Creator, "Master of the World, this great Light that is hidden with You, who is it for?" and the Creator answered that it was for those who would put an end to the Satan, Satan was stunned. He had thought that his work of inflicting pain, suffering, and death would last forever. The Creator invited the Satan to see for himself, and when the Angel of Death saw this great Light, he fell on his face. What the Creator revealed to the Angel of Death was the secret: "He will elevate himself and he will elevate his generation." This refers to the *Mashiach*, the Messiah. According to the *Midrash*, this was the moment when the Satan first came to the realization that immortality for humankind was inevitable.

My father, the Rav, always says that *Mashiach* is not a person; *Mashiach* is a certain consciousness. If we continue in our spiritual work but do not push ourselves to achieve audacity, *azut*, we will overlook the key to revealing this consciousness, this Light, and we will miss an opportunity to accelerate the process of bringing an end to pain, suffering, and darkness in the world.

In Vayigash, Yehuda was able to bring an end to the pain of his entire family, not because his spirit was so elevated but because he had awakened the holy audacity within himself. One of the gifts of the Shabbat of Vayigash is that it gives us access to the consciousness of Yehuda, helping those of us who desire the ability to awaken this *azut* within ourselves. Fortunately, we are all capable of summoning the *chutzpah*, the audacity to say, "I am going to ask for something that will elevate others." The Maccabees did it. Nakdimon did it. Yehuda did it. On the Shabbat of Vayigash, we are reminded that we, too, can play a part in bringing an end to pain, suffering, and darkness, but only, as the *Midrash* says, when we "raise ourselves up."

* * *

One day, Rabbi Aharon of Karlin received a message that he needed to go to a remote village to pray. So he gathered a few of his students and set off early the next day. The journey was long, and it was almost night before Rabbi Aharon and his students arrived at their destination. An old man answered their knock at the door of the village inn. "I've been waiting for you," he said. "Please come in."

Rabbi Aharon and his students entered the inn, and because of the late hour, began their evening prayers. As he prayed, Rabbi Aharon came to understand that he had been called to reveal a tremendous amount of Light in this town. So he and his students began to pray lustily, singing and dancing and calling out their fervent prayers.

They made so much noise that they roused the sleeping villagers. Hearing cries, the villagers assumed there must be a fire. In those days before fire departments, everyone worked together to put out a fire. On this night, when the villagers got up out of their beds, dashed to the well, and ran toward the inn with their buckets of water, they found all the windows open and saw people dancing and singing inside. Caught up in the fervor and enthusiasm of Rabbi Aharon and his students, the villagers quickly joined in the prayers.

As the prayers progressed into a feast of food and drink, so much joy and Light was being revealed that the students of Rabbi Aharon observed that this night had the taste of *Mashiach*, the Messiah, and of the Final Redemption. The next day, as Rabbi Aharon and his students prepared to leave the village, they bade the old man to say goodbye. He said, "I want you to know that today is my one hundred and seventh birthday. A hundred years ago, when my father owned this very inn, the Baal Shem Tov and his students came to spend the night. They did just as you and your students did last night. They prayed. They sang and danced, and the whole town joined them. When the Baal Shem Tov was about to leave, he turned to me, gave me a blessing, and said, 'One hundred years from now, another great spiritual master will come here with his students, and they are going to do as we have done. Make sure you tell them I was here before you.'"

Everything we do in our spiritual work has been done by someone before us. Yehuda was here before us, and he stood up for his brother. The *Hashmonaim* who came before us were unwilling to sit quietly in the face of oppression. Nakdimon ben Guryon, who stood up to ask the Creator for not one but two miracles, also came before us. We are not being asked to create a path where there is none, nor are we awakening anything new. We are simply finding trails to the miraculous that the spiritual giants of history have blazed for us.

The *Tana Devei Eliyahu*, an early *Midrash* attributed to the teachings of Elijah the Prophet, invites us to ask ourselves when our actions will achieve the level of Abraham, Isaac, and Jacob. We know we cannot create miracles or bring the Final Redemption on our own, but those spiritual giants who passed this way before us have paved the way for us, just as Yehuda does on the Shabbat of Vayigash. How do we achieve holy audacity? We do it by reminding ourselves that our actions reawaken what those before us accomplished, that we are only reconnecting to what they did. Because they opened up this channel for us, we can create miracles.

VAYECHI

The Baal Shem Tov tells us that it is no coincidence when different topics we study relate to each other: It is a sign from the Creator. Similarly, there are no coincidences when it comes to the Bible: Specific word choices are always significant. The Torah portion of Vayechi, which means "And he lived," underscores the point that Jacob did not merely pass seventeen years in Egypt. According to the *Zohar*, Jacob was not truly living his life prior to this time. Before entering Egypt, Jacob's days had been marked by pain and sadness. Only during his time in Egypt did he learn, to his great joy, that his long-lost son, Joseph, was alive and thriving as second-in-command to Pharaoh. In Egypt, Jacob would see all his children and grandchildren—seventy family members—alive and well.

Rabbi Shmuel Bornsztain, also known as the *Shem Mishmuel*, says we can understand how people on a lower spiritual level might not be considered to be living, according to the Torah. But how can we identify this concept with Jacob? Jacob, a highly elevated soul, was always connected to the Light of the Creator, so how can we say that during the first years of his life he did not "live?"

In *Likutei Torah*, Rav Isaac Luria, the Ari, says that the years that Jacob lived in Israel were years when Jacob's spiritual work was correcting the sin of Adam and the damage it did to the *Brit*, or Covenant, between God and man. Signs of that damage include heaviness and lack of what we call *chiut*, or excitement, which can be seen both in the person who has done the damage (Adam) and in the person correcting that harm (in this case, Jacob), but to some degree, this correction is something we all take on in this life. The Ari says that the amount of joy we have in our life is a good indication of whether we have corrected this damage or not. If we feel joy and excitement in our prayers and on Shabbat and in our connection to the *Zohar*, then we know that we have completed our part of this correction; if we do not feel that exuberance, we know that there is still more work to be done.

Because Jacob was purer than almost anyone who ever lived, he took it upon himself to spend a hundred and thirty years correcting Adam's damage, which meant that Jacob had to take on the manifestation of that damage as well: a life heavy with sadness. Jacob took upon himself the damaged *ibur*, or soul, of Adam so that he could correct it. After a hundred and thirty years, the Creator said that Jacob had done enough. Now he could live the next seventeen years taking joy in his family.

The *Zohar* poses a rhetorical question: Why did Jacob have to suffer so much? Why didn't Jacob see right away that Joseph was alive? After all, an elevated soul like Jacob had access to the power of *Ruach HaKodesh*, or Divine Inspiration. The *Zohar*'s answer is that the *Shechinah*, the manifestation of the Divine Presence closest to our world, could not abide with Jacob during all those years that he was in pain, during all those years that Joseph was away from his father, because the *Shechinah* cannot rest where there is pain and sadness. Therefore, because Jacob did not have complete Divine Inspiration, he could not see that Joseph was alive. Jacob did not know that the traumatic events he experienced—losing his beloved son, running away from his brother, and fighting with his father-in-law—were connected to the *tikkun* of Adam that Jacob had taken upon himself. The Creator never made this clear to Jacob, since this lack of clarity was also part of the correction.

Jacob's struggle to complete his correction was made far more difficult by doubt, brought on by the fact that he was working so hard spiritually and at a very high level, and yet his life was full of tragedy. Often, in our ignorance, we do not understand why certain things occur. "I'm doing so much good spiritual work," we say, "so how could this terrible thing befall me?" Rabbi Yitzchak Isaac of Komarna writes that when we experience strong doubts, this means a Divine judgment is coming down on us or on our family. If we succumb to those doubts, then we allow that judgment to manifest in our life, but if we fight off those doubts, we remove the judgment. How we choose to deal with doubt makes all the difference!

One evening after Shabbat, while a great kabbalist sat in meditation, one of his students brought him something warm to drink. The kabbalist's eyes were closed, and he was obviously deep in thought. After an hour, the drink got cold, so his student brought him another. This drink, too, got cold. When the student brought the kabbalist a third cup of something warm to drink, he saw his teacher open his eyes. So the student asked him, "What were you thinking about? What thoughts could be so engrossing that three times you failed to notice I was bringing you something hot to drink?"

The teacher answered, "Every Friday night, the perfect part of our soul comes down into our world. When Shabbat comes to an end, our everyday soul asks the perfect soul, 'Did I achieve anything; did I correct anything?' If the answer is yes, both parts of the soul rejoice. But if the answer is no, they both begin weeping inconsolably."

The kabbalist continued, "Every Shabbat, through our connection to our *Neshamah Yetara*, Additional Soul, we are given the ability to make a correction and to release the joy that comes with that correction. If we do not awaken this joy, the perfect part of our soul leaves. It is only through joy that we draw a little part of that perfected soul to us."

For a hundred and thirty years, Jacob's life was marked by sadness. But once he moved to Egypt, once he had completed his correction, Jacob could let go of the heaviness that he carried for so much of his life. Now he could truly live. Each of us comes into this life with a *tikkun*, a correction we must take on. Avoiding that work can lead to depression, and even when we engage in it, our doubts and uncertainties can contribute to our pain. But once we recognize what we are here to correct and succeed at the hard work of clearing away our *tikkun*, those thorny thickets give way to lush meadows, and sorrow gives way to exuberance and joy, just as it did for Jacob.

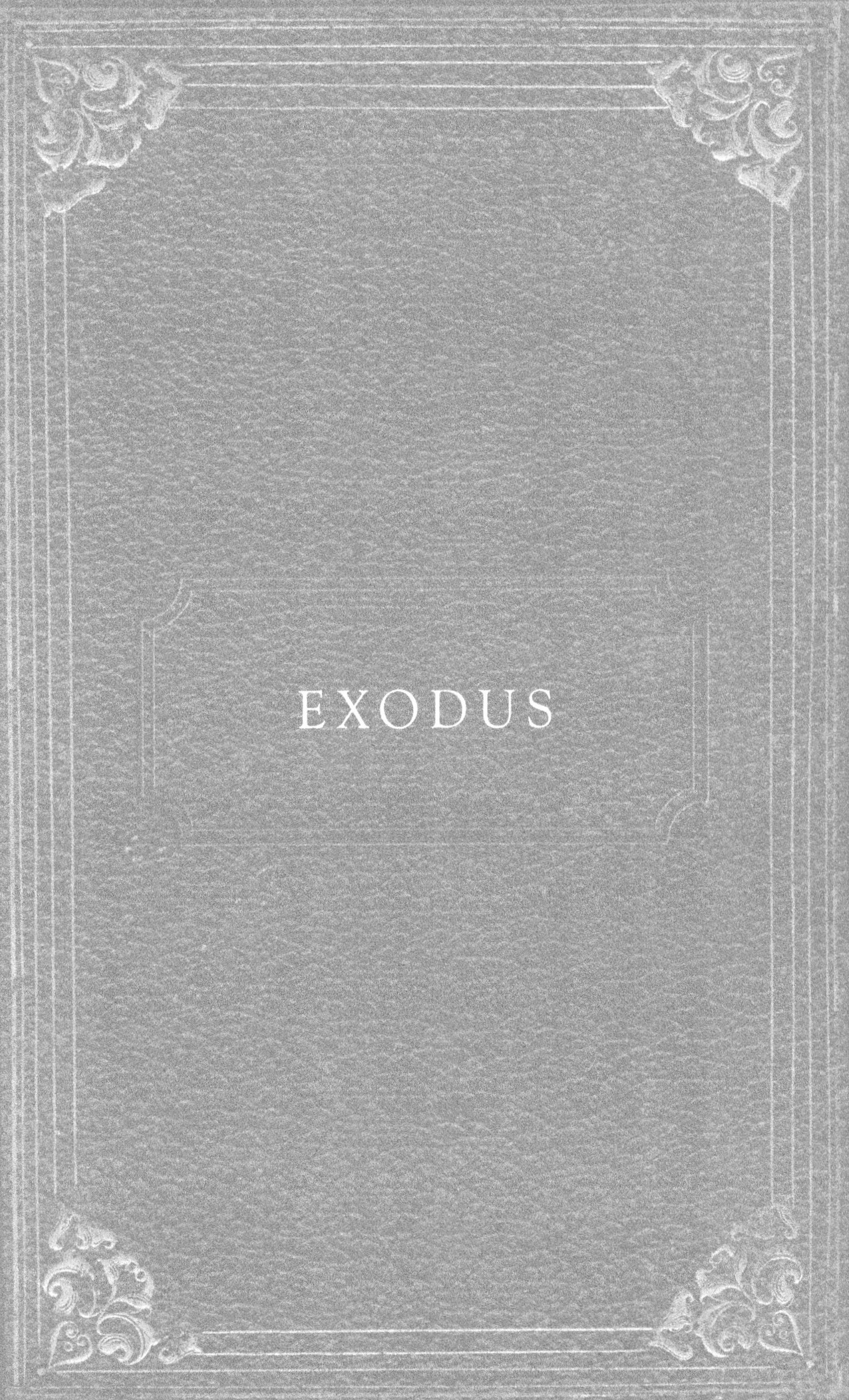
EXODUS

SHEMOT

The Bible tells us that the infant Moses was taken from the Nile River into the house of Pharaoh, where he was raised by the royal family. Many years later, Moses fled to Midian, became a shepherd, and married Tziporah, the daughter of Jethro, high priest of Midian. One day, while tending his flock of sheep in the desert, Moses saw a burning thorn bush on a nearby mountainside and climbed up to investigate. When Moses drew near the bush, the Creator was revealed to him.

Although Moses' decision to seek out the burning bush seems insignificant, given the more dramatic parts of this story, it is a crucially important moment, for Moses would not have encountered the Creator, had he not investigated the small fire in the distance. This action also reveals the state of Moses' consciousness—his awareness that nothing comes into our lives by accident, that everything that comes to our attention contains a sign from the Creator. So when Moses spotted the burning bush on the mountain, he knew it had special meaning: Something would be revealed to him there, so he climbed up to see what it might be.

How many of us would respond this way if we saw something out of the ordinary, the contemporary equivalent of a small fire off in the distance? Most of us would decide that it had nothing to do with us, and we'd continue going about our business. Why isn't the truth as clear to us as it was to Moses? The answer is that our consciousness has not yet reached the spiritual level where we truly understand that there are no coincidences. And because we do not see the Creator in everything, the Creator's messages are not always revealed to us.

This insight into the consciousness of Moses serves as a valuable reminder of just how often we're missing opportunities in life when we choose to ignore things happening around us, when we just pass them by. Imagine how different things might have been if Moses had thought, *It's just another desert fire*, and had kept on his way!

After Moses arrives at the burning thorn bush, the Creator appears to Moses and tells him that the suffering of the Israelites will soon come to an end, for Moses has been chosen to bring the Children of Israel out of Egypt. How does Moses respond to this miraculous, overwhelming moment? Astonishingly, he resists the Creator, offering one reason after another why he cannot agree to do God's bidding. So what are we to make of this?

Moses never doubts that it is God speaking to him; he never considers that he might be suffering hallucinations from the heat. Moses recognizes the Creator, and he knows how important God's plan could be to the Israelites. Yet Moses continues to find reasons for not acceding to the Creator's request. (Can you imagine how much restraint this must have required on God's part?)

Just when it seems that God has addressed all of Moses' concerns, Moses raises one more complication: He is "slow of speech and tongue," and surely someone without speech impediments would be better suited to persuade the Israelites to demand their freedom—and to cajole Pharaoh into giving it to them. Even after the Creator says He will guide Moses' speech, Moses continues to resist.

Rabbi Chaim ben Attar, the *Or HaChaim*, gives us precious insight into the discussion between Moses and the Creator. He asks why Moses mentions his speech impediment only at the end of this dialogue? It is not as if Moses had not already considered this obstacle. The fact of his being so inarticulate must have loomed large in Moses' life. But according to the *Or HaChaim*, when Moses first heard the Creator's plan, he just assumed that the Creator would heal him. Why would He not, if He wanted Moses to be His messenger? However, as his discussion with God continues and Moses sees that his speech impediment is not being removed, he decides it is time to raise the matter with the Creator.

The *Or HaChaim* tells us that the Creator replies by chiding Moses for his lack of faith. If Moses had less doubt, the Creator would have been able to work a healing miracle. But now, as a result of his doubts, Moses will have to continue to endure his awkward, stumbling speech. Only when the Creator needs Moses to speak on His behalf will Moses' speech be perfect. The moment that Moses finishes conveying the Creator's messages, his speech impediment will return. And this is exactly what happens. For the rest of his life, Moses stutters and stammers, except for those times when the Creator sends him to speak to the Israelites or to Pharaoh. On these occasions, Moses speaks without the slightest impediment. In fact, when speaking on the Creator's behalf, Moses is able to deliver the most remarkably moving and articulate speeches.

With the help of the *Or HaChaim*, the biblical portion of Shemot provides us with special insight into the terrible cost of doubt. A miracle could be on its way to us, but if we give way to our doubts, we can push that miracle away. Doubt will always present itself as a choice. In fact, the greater the miracle may be, the more room there will be for doubt.

Many of us have reasons—conscious or unconscious—for why we place limits on what we can accomplish, on how much we can help people. Once, while we studied together, my father, the Rav, explained that everything in the Tree of Life consciousness of the Upper Worlds is unimaginably different from what we expect in this world of the Tree of Knowledge of Good and Evil. When our experience and our preconceptions don't match up, we open the door to doubt. But when we see ourselves giving in to that doubt, we can remind ourselves of the portion of Shemot. We can bring Moses to mind and benefit both from his mistakes and from the miracle of freedom that he was able to bring forth for his people.

So how did Moses come by his speech problem? The *Midrash* says that Pharaoh knew that an Israelite male would become the leader who would free the Israelites. This was why he decreed that all male Israelite children be killed. Batya, Pharaoh's daughter, found Moses floating on the river and took him into her home. Thinking that Moses might be the child destined to free the Israelites, Pharaoh put him to a test. He set before the infant two piles: One of gold and silver coins, and another of hot coals. If Moses was to become a great leader, then surely, even as a baby, he would choose to reach for the gold and silver, rather than burn himself with the hot coals.

Had Moses reached for the gold and silver, Pharaoh would have had him killed on the spot. The *Midrash* explains that as Moses crawled toward the gold and silver coins, the Angel Gabriel took the baby's hand, placed it on a hot coal, and put the coal in Moses' mouth. It burned him badly, which led to his impaired speech. But why did the Creator cause Pharaoh to test Moses, knowing that this test would harm the child? The Creator did so to convey to us that the greatest teacher and leader in the history of humanity was a person with ordinary flaws, just like you and me.

I find this tremendously inspiring. Any time we have doubts about what we can do—doubts about our worthiness or our ability to help ourselves and others—we need only think about Moses. If we truly understand this teaching, we will see that we are up to the task. No limitation should ever make us think we are not enough, for any one of us—even someone whose ability to communicate has been compromised—can become one of the greatest leaders of all time.

VA'ERA

The biblical portion of Va'era begins with the Creator's revelation to Moses: "I am God." The Name of God used here is the *Yud, Hei, Vav,* and *Hei,* the Tetragrammaton, which represents a very high level of revelation and Light. The Creator goes on to say, "I appeared to Abraham, Isaac, and Jacob, but by this Name, I did not make myself known to them." To Moses, however, the Creator is revealing a greater Light.

Why does the revelation of the higher Name of God occur in the portion of Va'era? Commentary addressing this question typically begins with the end of the previous portion of Shemot. At the conclusion of that first portion in the Book of Exodus, Moses tells the Creator that the suffering of the Israelites has only become worse since Moses spoke to Pharaoh, prompting the *Zohar* to ask, "Who can speak to the Creator this way?" The *Zohar* goes on to explain that Moses was not satisfied with the level of Light being revealed to him. He was unwilling to settle for the lesser Light represented by the

Name *Adonai*, which connects to the lower level of *Malchut*, and it was in response to this request that the Creator agreed to reveal himself at the level of *Yud*, *Hei*, *Vav*, and *Hei*.

There is an important distinction between this explanation provided by the *Zohar* and the typical commentary. Most commentators believe the Creator was unhappy with Moses for reporting that the plight of the Israelites had grown worse, not better, since Moses had intervened. They say that this is why the Creator told Moses, "I want you to know that I have given more to you than I gave to your forefathers." But according to the *Zohar*, the Creator was *not* upset, for He knew that the impatience of Moses was working to the benefit of the Israelites. By demanding more from the Creator from the moment He named Himself, Moses successfully pushed Him to reveal a higher level of His Light.

The *Zohar* indicates that the Shabbat of Va'era marks a time when we can say to the Creator that we are not willing to accept the Light we are being offered. This is the time to tell the Creator that we know the Creator plans for the Redemption to happen sometime in the future, but we want it now. On the Shabbat of Va'era, we are given an opportunity to say *no*—even to something good—in order to ask for something better. The *Zohar* says that we draw from the strength of Moses when we do not accept what the Creator is offering us, when we press the Creator for more. Moses believed there were two paths the Israelites could take: The first is *be'ita*, the process that would lead to the Messiah coming at the allotted time; the other is *achishena*, or making things come faster. Needless to say, Moses preferred the latter.

Moses said to the Creator that if the Israelites did not hear him, how would Pharaoh? The Torah tells us that the Israelites could not hear

Moses. Their suffering in slavery was so great that it kept Moses' revelation from getting through. Moses was the right conduit, yet the Israelites could not accept this Light because they were so overworked and dispirited.

So how do we overcome doubts and allow miracles to occur? We can find some answers in a story about Elisha the Prophet. Elisha was in a desperate situation, for the king of Aram was intent on killing both Elisha and his apprentice, Gehazi. One morning, the two men awoke to find the army of Aram had surrounded them. Gehazi did not know what to do, but his master took Gehazi's hand and asked him what he saw. Gehazi replied that he could see angels surrounding the mountain to protect them. Then a miracle occurred: The sun grew so bright that it blinded the soldiers of Aram, who could no longer see the two men they had come to kill.

If Elisha could miraculously blind the soldiers, why did he need to first show Gehazi the vision of angels surrounding the mountain? Again, we return to the theme of trust. If a person does not have the consciousness of certainty in a miracle, the miracle cannot manifest. In this case, Elisha's power to bring about the miracle would have been neutralized by the doubt awakened by Gehazi. So Elisha showed him the ring of angels, which allowed Gehazi to believe that a miracle of protection would take place.

We find another lesson in the consciousness required for miracles in the biblical story of the Shunamite woman who turned to Elisha when her son died, asking the prophet to restore him to life. The Shunamite woman did not tell her husband where she was going or why because she knew that his lack of certainty would undermine the resurrection of his own son. This is why Moses said to the Creator, "If the miracle needs to happen for the Israelites and they cannot accept it, if their doubt is awakened, then there is no way the miracle can occur." As my father, the Rav, always says, "It is all about consciousness."

The *Midrash* asks why it was Aaron and not Moses who created the miracle of the first plague, the Plague of Blood? Why did the Creator tell Moses to instruct Aaron to take his stick and strike the Nile River? Rabbi Shlomo Yitzchaki, Rashi, explains that when Moses' mother placed the baby Moses in a basket on the Nile River, the river protected him. Moses therefore owed a debt of gratitude to the Nile River and thus could not be the one to hit it.

You may read this and think, "What feelings can the Nile River possibly have? Is it really going to hurt the Nile River's *feelings* if Moses hits it?" Once again, we are being provided with insight into the nature of consciousness. The sensitivity of Moses to the Nile River helps us see that there is consciousness in *everything* in our world. All objects—animate *and* inanimate—are connected through a network of energy, of Light. It was not only the *waters* of the Nile that saved Moses when he was floating downriver as a baby, it was also the *energy* within the Nile that saved him.

There are four levels of life: Inanimate, vegetable, animal, and human. Everything in our world is alive, even a table. Developing awareness of the constant interaction between ourselves and everything around us helps us complete our *tikkun*, the correction that is the reason we were born into this lifetime. Throughout his life, Moses needed assistance from such objects as water, rocks, and wooden staffs; he was constantly interacting with inanimate objects. Most of us, however, are unaware of the role inanimate objects play in our own spiritual development and growth.

My father, the Rav, makes the point that when we choose a loaf of *challah* for the right-hand side of the table at our Shabbat meal (this being the loaf we cut and eat after the blessing) and put an even nicer loaf on the left-hand side, it is important not to switch these two loaves. Why? Because now the *challah* on the right-hand side has the consciousness that it is going to be used for the *HaMotzi* (the blessing over the bread), and to change this would be awkward for it. To some of us, this might sound trivial or even silly, but we want this *challah* to give us its energy on this Shabbat. If we switch the *challah* and thereby embarrass it, we will receive less Light from this important connection.

The *Zohar* says that just as our *challah* thinks about us, so do our clothes and all other things. If we do them any harm, everything else in the inanimate kingdom will know about it and will not help us, for the entire realm of inanimate objects is in constant communication with itself as well as with all living things. We cannot achieve our *Gemar HaTikkun* without the assistance of all four aspects of life, so we must strive to be respectful of everything in the kingdom, whether it is inanimate, vegetable, animal, or human.

With the support of all things, we can move closer to certainty. On the Shabbat of Va'era, Moses approaches the Creator and asks how he can bring about the *Gemar HaTikkun* if the Israelites don't listen to him. Moses is not just speaking here about the Israelites of his time; he is speaking about us, too. Without the consciousness of certainty, how can we hope to escape the chariots of mighty Pharaoh? How can we overcome the forces of death and bring about *bila hamavet lanetzach*, the death of death?

Without certainty, we just can't do it. So how can we arrive at certainty? We do so by looking for the truth that lies beyond the mere appearance of things, much the same way we parse the words of the Torah. Isaiah the Prophet explains that prior to the *Gemar HaTikkun*, the Final Correction, there has to be some level of concealment, so we must find a way to see through it. One of the great gifts of the Shabbat of Va'era is that we can awaken the strength of Moses by not accepting things as they are (or seem to be), and by treating all things with respect. When we see the world of greater possibilities, when we look beyond the surface to the greater truth that lies behind the veils of concealment, our doubts become certainty, and miracles become possible.

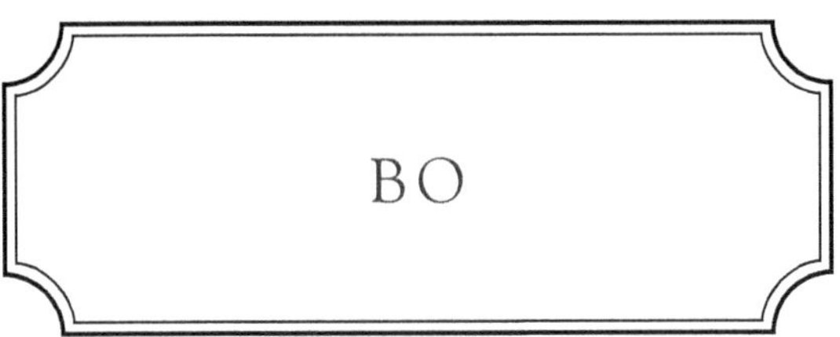

BO

One evening, while studying the teachings of the sages, I found myself wondering what Rabbi Kalonymus Kalman Shapira, the *Esh Kodesh*, had to say about the biblical portion of Bo. Descendant of a long line of distinguished kabbalists, the *Esh Kodesh* taught and was killed during the Holocaust. Miraculously, both his writings and his teachings survived and have since been published. I turn to them often as a source of clarity and inspiration.

The *Zohar* says that the Creator is revealed to us according to how much we are *aware* that the Creator is being revealed to us, which means that the Creator's role in our lives is limited only by our ignorance. In truth, He is revealing Himself to us all the time. Moses knew this, which is why he sought out the thorn bush burning on the mountainside. If we truly believe the Creator is being revealed to us right now, the Creator *will* be revealed to us right now, much the way He was revealed to Moses.

So why don't we all just overthrow our ignorance, now that we know this is our only limitation? The reason is simple, though deeply rooted: Our self-serving actions stand in the way—stumbling blocks between us and this life-changing shift in consciousness. We cannot replace ignorance with the certainty of the Creator's presence because we cannot see through the darkness we draw to ourselves through our ego-based actions. Instead of seeing the Creator in all things, we see ourselves (and behave accordingly).

The *Esh Kodesh* makes two important points about how we can develop this vital aspect of our spiritual work—our certainty. First, he tells us that according to the *Zohar*, there is only Light and darkness, meaning that recognizing falsehood is as crucial as seeing the truth. Secondly, he says we have to realize that everything of a *spiritual nature* is a revelation of the Light of the Creator, which reminds us that we need to make an all-important distinction between physical desire and spiritual desire. Let's take a moment to explore this second point.

We have many desires, both physical and spiritual. Our desire for food and drink, for example, is physical. When we feel the urge to eat a steak, we rightly think of this desire as our own. The mistake we make is applying this same understanding to our *spiritual* desires; we believe that when we have the desire to pray or to share or to help, that this desire is *also* our own.

Fulfilling any desire involves a three-step process: First, the desire is awakened within us, then we act on it, and finally we succeed in accomplishing whatever satisfies that desire. But as the *Esh Kodesh* tells us, we need to be aware that when it comes to spiritual desires, the first step is *not* ours—it comes from the Creator. I woke up today and wanted to pray, not because *I* desired it but because the Creator came to me this morning, just as He did centuries ago to the prophets Moses, Isaiah, and Jeremiah—and just as He does to you. The *Esh Kodesh* says that although most of us do not have visions like those of the prophets, eventually, with God's help, we may. In the meantime, our visions come in the form of feelings. To the prophets, the Creator said, "I am putting My Word in your mouth." For those of us who are not prophets, it is not God's Word that He places in our mouth: It is His Desire that He places in our soul.

Daniel the Prophet acknowledged this when he said, "I saw the vision, and those who were with me did not, yet suddenly they became afraid." Emotion is a lower level of revelation, which is why it was the experience of those around Daniel, who were not as spiritual as he was. When we wake up in the morning and the Creator comes to us and says, "I am putting My Desire in your heart," most of us do not actually see the Creator, surrounded by all the angels, coming to awaken our soul. Instead, like those who traveled with Daniel, we have a feeling. Only in this case, it is not fear but a renewed sense of spiritual purpose. When we become aware of this truth and own it, we see that not one morning goes by without the Creator coming to us and saying, "Here is My Desire for you today." Our job is to pay attention so we don't miss the Creator's appearance.

The *Maor VaShemesh*, Rabbi Kalonymus Kalman Halevi Epstein, one of the students of Rabbi Elimelech of Lizhensk, says that when we talk about the secrets of the Torah, we are not talking about the *Zohar* or the writings of the Ari because whoever wants to can read and understand them. They are not secrets; they are prophecy. The true secrets of the Torah are the personal revelations the Creator awakens in each of us. Every person has a different revelation of the Light of the Creator while reading and studying the *Zohar*, depending on their level of spiritual growth. The *Esh Kodesh* suggests that after any spiritual activity, including Shabbat, we take a moment or two to ask ourselves whether we connected to the feeling intended by the Creator. This allows the awareness that everything is from the Creator to play a consistent role in our daily lives. So when I thought, "I wonder what the *Esh Kodesh* has to say about the portion of Bo," this was not *my* thought. It was the Creator asking me to look into the *Esh Kodesh*'s teachings.

In a way, we're talking about a self-fulfilling prophecy (I don't mean "prophecy" in the spiritual sense here). When we have a sudden desire to open up the *Zohar* and we think it is *our* own thought, it *becomes* our thought, which keeps its power limited. As we come to realize it is the Creator's Thought that has awakened our desire to open the *Zohar*, we become more and more open to personal revelation. And with this growth comes an increased sense of certainty, which allows us to reveal even more Light.

One of the great lessons of the portion of Bo is that although the Creator can be found in all things, the decision to look for Him lies in our hands. To do so, however, we have to make a shift in consciousness. Eventually, when we no longer question whether or not we are seeing the Hand of the Creator, when we acknowledge that absolutely every thought of a spiritual nature is a direct revelation from the Creator, we will begin to rise to the level of the prophets.

How we think about our feelings also affects how much certainty we have, which in turn determines if those feelings reveal the Light of the Creator. So if we have a feeling and act on it, but we are not sure whether this is the Creator's impulse or our own, darkness can enter our lives. However, even if we are not sure, we can still choose to awaken the power of certainty, for if we realize that every single feeling of awakening comes directly from the Creator, then there is no opening for doubt. We can encourage this awakening consciousness within ourselves, not only for our own good but for the benefit of the entire world.

The *Esh Kodesh* says that in certain situations, we have the ability to reveal and receive Light *beyond* our ordinary capacity—even when that capacity is enhanced by our awareness of the presence of the Creator. We've already seen one example of this: When we study a spiritual text on our own, we can receive a certain revelation of the Light, but when we study together in unity, we can experience a new level of awakening, well beyond our individual understanding. But that's not all. The *Esh Kodesh* tells us that when we teach others for the purpose of revealing Light, the Creator gives us additional revelations as well.

The revelation given to a teacher has three levels. The first is personal, and after this a teacher receives two additional degrees of insight: One reveals what the student needs right now, and the other points out exactly what the student will need next. Knowing that when we teach we are given these three revelations, we need to be alert to them—and we must always acknowledge their source. If we fall back into thinking that it is we who are doing all the teaching, we slide into darkness, robbing ourselves and our students of this chance at additional Light.

The *Esh Kodesh* explored these remarkable themes during the Holocaust. Imagine what it must have been like to experience the power of the Creator to bring Light into darkness at this most terrible period in human history. The timing was no coincidence, however. When Rav Ashlag was asked why he was writing his commentary on the *Zohar* during the Second World War when there were so many terrible dangers, he replied, "From the greatest darkness comes the greatest revelation." And so it was for the *Esh Kodesh*, too.

The Bible says something beautiful in Malachi: "The lips of a priest will keep the wisdom, and from his mouth they will ask for direction, for he is an angel of God." This verse tells us that when we take on the task of teaching spiritual lessons, the Creator reveals His Wisdom through us. We can become angels right now, if we have the correct consciousness when we teach, at least for the time that we are teaching. We can elevate this way because what we do is not for ourselves. In the portion of Shemot, the Creator gave Moses the ability to speak clearly while giving voice to prophecy, but when Moses was not speaking on the Creator's behalf, his speech impediment returned. Many of us can be angels of God when we teach, so long as we remember that we serve in this way as conduits for the Creator.

The *Esh Kodesh* goes on to say, "When we repeat the words of Torah from a righteous person, the righteous person's lips move in the grave." The word used here is "lips," not "mouth," because even a righteous teacher is only a vehicle for the revelations of the Creator. The deeper point is that when we repeat the words of a righteous person's teachings, we connect directly to the revelation that the teacher gave to his students while the teacher was in this world. The Rav said that Rav Ashlag, for example, taught from a level even higher than that of the prophets, so by repeating the words that the Creator gave Rav Ashlag, we, too, can connect to this otherwise unattainable level.

This portion of the Torah is named Bo, which means "come," referring to the first verse: "Then the Lord said to Moses, 'Come to Pharaoh, for I have hardened his heart.'" The Torah says that when the Creator made this demand of Moses, the two were in Egypt, which prompts the commentators to ask how this could be. If Moses considered Egypt so spiritually dark that he would not even pray in that country, how could the Creator reveal Himself to Moses there? Now that we have learned that from the greatest darkness comes the greatest revelation, we can begin to see how this could happen.

No matter how deeply mired we are in our own Egypt, according to the *Esh Kodesh*, a unique channel opens up each year on the Shabbat of Bo thanks to the revelation of Moses and Aaron who act as conduits for the Creator. By offering insight into the nature of revelation and by providing the services of Moses and Aaron as direct channels to the Creator, the portion of Bo and the Shabbat of Bo give us access to Light when we most need it.

I would like to end this discussion of the portion of Bo with this excerpt from the diary of Rabbi Kalonymus Kalman Shapira, the *Esh Kodesh*:

> *My thoughts have become weak, and I am about to become mute and to fall. Friday night after the meal, I came back and no one paid attention. So I went home and I opened up my window and looked out into the world. With all of my heart, I called out to the Creator. I opened up the window and yelled out, "Shema Yisrael, HaShem Elokeinu, HaShem Echad [God is one]." And then it was as if I saw the entire world shake. I began to say, "Adon Olam, asher Malach [Everything is made by the Creator, everything is the Creator]." And I saw that the entire world was swallowing up all the words coming out of my heart and mouth. My heart and my soul became strong. All my thoughts and the source of my thoughts and*

my feelings became alive again, both in the house and outside. Even if I think people are listening to me, and even if they are not, I will still at least speak—if not to people, I will speak to the world. And if I can make the world holy, maybe even the people living in the world can also become holy. And they will start singing the praises and understanding of this world.

BESHALACH

While paging through the *Zohar* to discover what unique gift is given to us on the Shabbat of Beshalach, I came across a section that reads as follows: "The energy of the words that come out of a person's mouth literally awakens the same type of energy from Above. If a person speaks good things, he awakens positive Light from Above. If a person speaks negatively, he awakens negative energy from Above." The *Zohar* goes on to make a specific suggestion: "If a person is participating and connecting to the Light of Shabbat, he should not awaken the mundane, for by doing so, he literally causes damage to the Light of Shabbat."

Twenty years ago, I was in Israel where my family and I had just spent all night visiting the graves of the truly righteous. When we returned to the hotel that morning, I was standing at the window of my room, unwrapping a stick of chewing gum, when suddenly I heard the solitary sound of a *Shofar*. I suddenly remembered the teaching that just before the arrival of the *Gemar HaTikkun*, the Final Correction a *Shofar* will be blown. My heart began to race, thinking that we must have revealed an amazing amount of Light the night before! Then I thought to myself, *How could I be unwrapping a stick of gum just before the Gemar HaTikkun? It cannot be.* And it wasn't. Not that time.

Why am I sharing this story with you? Because very few of us take how we behave seriously enough, including me. Chewing gum is just the sort of mundane activity that the *Esh Kodesh* warned against, especially during a deeply spiritual moment like mine when I was still glowing from my contact with the spirits of great sages. Even the smallest actions and words contain energy. If we deflate the moment with mundane thoughts and actions, we turn down the Light, but when we act thoughtfully and speak affirmatively, we inspire a surge of positive energy.

A number of amazing things happen in the portion of Beshalach, including the parting of the Red Sea. Just prior to that miracle, the Creator said to the Israelites, "I will do battle, and you must remain silent," which indicates that on this Shabbat, the power of words is even greater than usual. The *Zohar* goes on to explain that the Light revealed on the Shabbat of Beshalach is called the Light of *Atika,* which is beyond anything we can awaken with our work or with our prayers. This is why the Creator warned the Israelites not to speak. If their words had awakened any other type of Light during the splitting of the Red Sea, they would have diminished the superior Light being revealed at that time, much the way mundane thoughts dampen the effect of the Light on Shabbat. On the Shabbat of Beshalach, even the Light revealed by prayer or study can diminish the greater Light available to us.

If the Light of this Shabbat is not revealed through spiritual work, then how is it revealed? To answer to this question, first we need to know that the kabbalists chose to name this day *Shabbat Shirah*, or "Shabbat of the Song." I find this surprising, don't you? When we look at the major events that took place at the parting of the Red Sea—the revelation of the 72 Names of God, the great miracle itself of the splitting of the Red Sea, and the song that the Israelites sang thanking the Creator for saving their lives—the song seems to be the *least* important event. Why not name this the "Shabbat of the Miracle of the Red Sea" instead of the "Shabbat of the Song"?

As we look closer, however, we see that song itself is a singular event in the Torah. The sages tell us that prior to the parting of the Red Sea, the only record of a song in the biblical history of Creation was when Adam gathered all the living creatures together and said, "Let us go and sing before the Creator." According to the *Midrash*, no one in the Bible had sung a song prior to the Israelites singing the Song of the Sea.

My father, the Rav, explains that in this life there are two realities, both of which exist at the same time. One is the reality of the Tree of Knowledge of Good and Evil, where, unfortunately, most of us reside, and the other is the reality of the Tree of Life. When we look at events in the physical world and see them as good or bad, we are living in the more superficial reality of the Tree of Knowledge of Good and Evil. In the deeper reality of the Tree of Life, there is only good. If we were able to look at our world today and see only goodness, we would be standing in the *Gemar HaTikkun*, the Final Correction. However, because we still live within the realm of the Tree of Knowledge of Good and Evil, we still see darkness as well as Light.

Ultimately, the purpose of our life in this world—the goal of all the work we accomplish and the spiritual levels we attain—is to elevate ourselves and the world to the consciousness of the Tree of Life reality, the consciousness that everything is good. The *Midrash* explains that when the Israelites sang as they crossed the Red Sea, the words came to them directly from the Creator, and their song gave voice to an extraordinary expression of unity. Surprisingly, the revelation of the 72 Names of God and the great miracle of the parting of the Red Sea were not as important as what the words of the Israelites' song made possible: An experience of Tree of Life consciousness, a taste of miraculous unity.

The Shabbat of Beshalach is the only Shabbat of the year where the consciousness of *Shirah*—of the unity of the world, of the Tree of Life—is revealed. This priceless gift cannot be successfully described: We have to experience it. This is why the *Zohar* makes it so clear that on the Shabbat of Beshalach, we have to be exceptionally careful of our speech—even our spiritual speech. This is a Shabbat when, if we are quiet, the experience of Tree of Life consciousness is made more available to each of us.

In the Haftarah of Beshalach from the Book of Judges, we read that Deborah the Prophetess told Barak ben Abinoam that she had a message for him from God. The message was that Barak would become a leader, and that he needed to go to Mount Tabor and gather an army of 10,000. Deborah explained to Barak that these men would come from the tribes of Naftali and Zebulun, and that once Barak had assembled them, a miracle would allow Barak to defeat Siserah, the general of the Canaanite army, in battle. Through Deborah, the Creator told Barak that this was Barak's chance to do what he came into this world to accomplish. But Barak was uncertain.

Barak did not doubt that the Creator spoke to him through Deborah, but he did not truly believe that he, on his own, could be a channel for victory. So he asked Deborah to accompany him and support him. Once he had made this decision, however, the Light of the Creator would not give him the strength he needed for a victory. Deborah had to accompany him in order to defeat the army of the Canaanites. As a result, while Deborah achieved the level of *Shirah*, the Tree of Life, Barak himself never achieved that consciousness on his own.

As we read this Haftarah on the Shabbat of Beshalach, we, too, have the opportunity to receive this revelation of Deborah the Prophetess. If Deborah were to come to us on the Shabbat of *Shirah* with a promise of the Creator's support, would we believe her? Would we accept her words as the truth? If our answer is yes, then we can achieve the level of *Shirah*, as the Israelites did at the Red Sea and as Deborah herself did. But if our answer is no, then, like Barak, we will not.

This lesson extends beyond the Shabbat of Beshalach; it holds true all throughout our lives. Our consciousness creates our reality. Do we know with certainty that if the Creator chooses us, we can become a complete channel for the Light of the Creator? If we do not, then, quite simply, that door is closed to us. The moment Barak said, "I do not think I can do it on my own," Deborah responded, "You are right. You cannot." Fortunately, we have another option. On the Shabbat of Beshalach, the Creator comes to each of us through Deborah and asks, "Do you accept that you can achieve the Tree of Life consciousness? Do you accept the task for which I have chosen you?" Those of us who say yes will have the gift of the Shabbat of Beshalach revealed to us.

On the Shabbat of Beshalach, the gates of the Tree of Life swing open. We cannot talk about it. We cannot study it. All we can do is experience it, for this is a Shabbat of consciousness. We have to feel the certainty that we can do it on our own, or we will fall spiritually like Barak. Yes, Barak accomplished great things, but nowhere near what he might have. On the Shabbat of Beshalach, we have to step into our boundless potential to elevate ourselves—and the rest of the world—to the Tree of Life reality.

YITRO

The title of this biblical portion, Yitro, "Jethro," refers to Moses' father-in-law. In this portion, the Creator gives Moses and Aaron the Torah (Ten Utterances); He offers the Israelites the greatest spiritual revelation of Light ever, and Yitro visits the camp of the Israelites. Just as we did in the previous portion, we have to ask why this *name* was chosen for it. If Moses was the channel for the Ten Utterances and the revelation of *bila hamavet lanetzach* (removal of death, immortality) on Mount Sinai, why is this portion called "Yitro" and not "Moshe"? What is so significant about Yitro that he merits having this Torah portion named after him, especially when Moses would be the far more obvious choice?

The *Zohar* says that what transpired spiritually with Yitro was a prerequisite to receiving immortality, so let's take a closer look at this idea. As we saw with Moses and the burning bush, when we are truly ready to connect to the Light of the Torah, we attain a state of elevated consciousness where everything that happens is significant.

The *Zohar* tells us that in this state, even the words of the negative person are seen as important, and even a destructive life like Yitro's can be seen to reveal Light to the rest of the world.

If someone like Yitro were to come to you or me and say, "I know you think you are doing a decent job, but actually you're not; let me tell you how to fix it," we would probably be put off, if not offended. In this biblical portion, however, we see that we put our spiritual selves at risk if we do not acknowledge the messages we receive from everyone. We cannot receive the Torah if we are not open to listening to anyone at any time. If we are fully aware that we should consider everything as if it were coming from the Creator, even when its source is a person who has done terrible things, then we are ready to receive the greatest spiritual revelation of all time.

Rav Mordechai Yosef Leiner of Izbica, the *Mei HaShiloach*, puts it this way: "The Torah does not say Moses listened to the *words* of Yitro, but to the *voice* of Yitro, and Moses did everything Yitro said." The *Mei HaShiloach* adds, "Yitro knew that what he was saying to Moses was of great importance, but he did not himself comprehend the message. Yitro did not understand the power of his connection to the true words of the Creator. However, Moses understood the totality of what Yitro said." There was an enormous spiritual divide between Moses and Yitro, yet Moses listened to, understood, and acted on the words of Yitro in their entirety, regardless of whether or not Yitro himself understood them. As Rabbi Zadok HaKohen Rabinowitz, the *Pri Tzadik* says, "Our spiritual work comes from everything we hear."

Rabbi Kalonymus Kalman Shapira, the *Esh Kodesh*, the great rabbi whose teachings were revealed during the Holocaust, explains that the soul of a righteous person is like a father to other souls. Most of us have a *Neshama pratit* (a private, personal soul), which reveals our own personal Light. But the soul of a truly righteous person, a *tzadik*, is so full of desire to give its Light to others that it can reveal more than just personal Light. The righteous soul creates a bank of spiritual Light that can be drawn down by anyone who desires to connect to the Light of that particular soul. Just as the sun nourishes the entire world, so, too, do righteous souls let their Light shine upon all who come close to them.

Rav Shimon bar Yochai's accomplishment in revealing the *Zohar* is as great as that of Moses in revealing the Torah at Mount Sinai, for the *Zohar* contains all the Light we need to bring about not only our own correction, but also the *Gemar HaTikkun*, the Final Correction. The problem is that we have allowed the Light of Rav Shimon bar Yochai to elevate a little too high, for the souls of the righteous are like helium balloons: If we don't hold onto their strings, they will float away from our world. Our goal, yours and mine, is to bring Rav Shimon's Light closer to the world through our spiritual work. By awakening a deep connection to the *Zohar*, we can draw down the Light of Rav Shimon bar Yochai, not only for ourselves but for the world.

In the *Sulam* of the *Zohar*, Rav Ashlag's commentary, he says we cannot elevate unless we receive an *ibur*, an implantation from the soul of a righteous person into our own. Without this *ibur*, we cannot grow. We can study all day and pray all day and night, but we will not elevate unless we merit assistance from the soul of a righteous person.

If a person's wisdom is greater than his or her spiritual actions, it cannot last because there is no Vessel to contain the Light he or she is revealing. When we reveal more Light than our Vessel can hold, the excess floats away. We can only hold on to the amount of Light that our Vessel can contain. The purpose, then, of our spiritual growth is to create a large enough Vessel so that all the Light we reveal can stay in the world. When we attach ourselves to the souls of the righteous, we become part of the Vessel that holds their Light, thereby keeping their Light in this world, too. Through the *Zohar*, we can hold onto the awesome Light of the *Zohar* and of Rav Shimon bar Yochai.

The *Zohar* explains that much of the Light of righteous souls like Rav Shimon bar Yochai is concealed from us. By not being able to see as they do—by not being able to see, for example, as Moses did, that everything, even the high priest of Midian, is a gift from the Creator—we're often stumbling blindly.

Rav Ashlag uses a parable to illustrate this point, in which a man dies, leaving behind a son who lives in darkness and terrible poverty. In fact, his father has left him a chest full of riches, but because the son is in the dark, he cannot see it. He walks around all day, banging into the walls of his dark house, crying out with pain and suffering, while all the time what he needs to prosper is right at hand. Every day, Rav Shimon bar Yochai and Rav Ashlag say to us, "It is here! The Light you need, the Light the world needs for the *Gemar HaTikkun*, is right here!" We cannot see it, but we can continue to work toward that moment of insight when everything is transformed, when we see and listen to everyone and everything with the openness of Moses.

MISHPATIM

The biblical portion of Mishpatim, with its details of the laws regarding slaves and animals, feels like a letdown after the dramatic story of Yitro, in which the Israelites leave Egypt, cross the Red Sea, receive the miracles of manna and water, and triumph over Amalek in their first battle. But the *Zohar* helps us understand the power of the Shabbat of Mishpatim by explaining that although the Bible appears to be describing mundane laws, it is actually providing us with a vision of what we must do to achieve the *Gemar HaTikkun*, the Final Correction.

The *Zohar* tells us that the Israelites received the gift of *bila hamavet lanetzach*, of immortality, at Mount Sinai, but because of the sin of the golden calf, they lost it and death swiftly restored its power in the world. The Creator told Moses then—and is telling us now—that we live in a world of *mishpatim*, of judgments. The obvious question for us is this: How can we remove the judgment that was passed on the world at Mount Sinai so that we can reopen the way for the *Gemar HaTikkun*?

The portion of Mishpatim begins with the words, *"Eile mishpatim,"* or "These are the judgments." *Mishpatim*, or judgments, represent the pain of the Creator. After the incident of the golden calf, the Creator tells Moses that the Israelites are in trouble; they were just recently given the ability to transcend the power of death, but they have already lost it. The Creator tells Moses that only way to remove the darkness brought about by building the golden calf is to make sure the Israelites bring down His pain into this world. The *Zohar* tells us that two tears wept by the Creator sustain our world because they contain the seeds of the Light of the Redemption. The *Esh Kodesh* explains that the weeping of the Creator is not simply for the pain of this world; it also holds within it the key to the removal of the pain of this world.

The portion of Mishpatim gives us an opening to draw the Light of the *Gemar HaTikkun* closer to our world by attuning ourselves to the pain of the Creator. When we make it a priority to beg the Creator to reveal His pain to us, we bring the *Gemar HaTikkun* that much closer to our world. However, as long as we are caught up in the pain of our own egos, we cannot feel the pain of the Creator. It is a difficult spiritual task to truly push aside all of our own imagined or real pain and ask to feel only the pain of the Creator, but since the golden calf was created, this has been one way to bring about the *Gemar HaTikkun.*

Most of us think that all we need to do is contribute our fair share to bringing about the *Gemar HaTikkun*, the end of pain and suffering in this world. Since others are involved in this work as well, we figure that some people will do a little more, others a little less, but together our contributions will tip the balance. But it doesn't work that way. Every person in this world has a specific job that nobody else can do. Unless we do ours, we will be holding everyone else back from the *Gemar HaTikkun.*

In a beautiful story in the *Midrash*, we learn that when the Israelites built the Temple, they chose only the most exquisite and perfect stones for its construction. There was one stone the builders thought was not good enough to be a part of the construction of the Temple, so they discarded it. However, when the time came to lay the final stone, which happened to be part of the Holy of Holies, there were no stones left. The builders were in a quandary, and then someone remembered the flawed stone. When it was set into the gap in the Holy of Holies, it fit perfectly. The Temple was now complete.

This lowliest of stones had assumed its rightful place in the most powerful spot of the Temple—the site that would draw the most Light of the Creator, the Holy of Holies. No matter how unimportant we may think we are, we all have an essential role to play in bringing about the *Gemar HaTikkun.*

TERUMAH

The *Zohar* tells us that the underlying message of Terumah is this: All the Creator wants for us is to truly desire His Light. Once we do this, everything becomes available. The Israelites were struggling to find materials to build the Tabernacle, but when they awakened within themselves a pure desire to give more than they were capable of giving, the Creator helped them. At its heart, the portion of Terumah is all about desire.

In preparation for building the Tabernacle, the Israelites gathered gold, silver, animal skins, and fabric. But Rabbi Isaiah ben Avraham HaLevi Horowitz, the *Shlah*, explains that even after collecting everything they could, the Israelites still did not have all the materials they needed. He tells us that according to the Torah, "The Creator instructed Moses, 'Speak to the Israelites, and tell them that they should take from Me a *terumah*.'" The word *terumah* is often translated as "charity" or "giving," so at first glance, it appears that the Israelites were being told to give something of their own. But this was not the case. The *Shlah* explains that the Creator's instruction to "*take* from Me a *terumah*" means that the Israelites were to take something that rightfully belonged to the Creator and contribute this to the building of the Tabernacle.

The *Shlah* adds that the Creator intended that the Israelites should give whatever they could of their own belongings and that Moses would then awaken their true desire to give more. Had the Israelites given only what they were physically capable of giving, without kindling their desire to do more, there would not have been material enough to build the Tabernacle. However, because their desire to give was strong and true, it was supported by the Creator. In other words, if the Israelites had only five pieces of gold but their inner desire was to give ten or fifteen pieces, the Creator saw to it that the amount of the gold they could contribute grew in accord with their desire.

One of the most important objects in the Tabernacle was the candelabrum, whose purpose was to emit the Light of the Creator for eternity. An interesting discussion took place between the Creator and Moses regarding the construction of the candelabrum. The *Talmud* says that at Mount Sinai, the Creator showed Moses a vision of the entire Tabernacle, inside and out, as well as how to build it and what materials would be needed. The Creator explained to Moses that the candelabrum was to be wrought from a single piece of gold, but Moses had difficulty understanding exactly how this would be done.

Although the Creator tried numerous times to help Moses see how to make the candelabrum, Moses still couldn't get it right. Finally the Creator revealed to Moses a candelabrum made of fire, to serve as a model. When the Creator saw that Moses was still unable to make the candelabrum, He said, "Throw the gold into the fire." The word the

Creator used in explaining what would happen was *te'ase*, or "will be made," implying that the candelabrum would make itself. Rabbi Shlomo ben Yitzchaki, Rashi, tells us that once Moses had flung the gold into the fire, a miracle took place and the candelabrum came into existence on its own.

Did the Creator not know that Moses was incapable of making the candelabrum? Of course, He knew. So why did the Creator spend so much time at Mount Sinai explaining the candelabrum's construction to Moses? Why didn't the Creator just tell Moses to throw the gold into the fire in the first place?

The *Zohar* tells us that this story in the portion of Terumah offers us special insight into the importance of desire. Desire is everything. If someone else had taken the gold and thrown it into the fire, nothing would have happened; it was Moses' true desire that the candelabrum should reveal the Light of the Creator that made the miracle possible. Although the Creator knew that Moses couldn't build the candelabrum on his own, He needed someone with Moses' tremendous desire to reveal the candelabrum's Light and to manifest this awesome tool in our world.

Many of us think it is we who accomplish what we make in this world, but Moses knew better. Moses knew he could only achieve true desire for the Light of the Creator. When we help someone, if we think it is we who are doing the work, we will accomplish very little. Only when we realize that we cannot do anything except awaken in ourselves true desire can the Creator step in and help. Then, and only then, do miracles become possible. The purpose of the discussion back and forth between the Creator and Moses at Mount Sinai was not to perfect Moses' ability to build the candelabrum, but to perfect his desire.

In this context, the *Zohar* poses a wonderful question: "How do we know if the Light of the Creator is in someone, or within us?" The *Zohar* explains that the only way to be sure is to sense the *desire* for the Light, either in ourselves or in someone else. What we know and how we act are not accurate indications of how connected we are to the Light of the Creator. A person can be amazingly successful or wise, yet have no connection to the Light of the Creator at all. The *Zohar* says the only way to recognize a connection to the Light of the Creator is to gauge the strength of the desire for that Light.

Anything lasting, anything true, can only manifest from true desire. This is the gift of the Shabbat of Terumah and specifically the gift of the third meal of every Shabbat during the year, eaten at the time of *et ratzon*, which means "awakening desire." Every Shabbat—but particularly on the Shabbat of Terumah—we need to ask the Creator to please give us an awakening of spiritual desire because this is the source of everything that is good and true.

TETZAVEH

On the Shabbat of Tetzaveh, we read two sections from the Torah. Not only do we read the Torah portion of Tetzaveh, which describes the Creator's ongoing instructions for the building of the Tabernacle, but there is an additional section from the portion of Ki Tetze (the sixth portion in the Book of Deuteronomy), known as Zachor, that we read as well. The word *zachor* means "to remember," and this additional reading tells the story of the defeat of the Israelites at the hands of the nation of Amalek, a defeat that represents a significant fall in consciousness.

The portion of Tetzaveh is almost always read on the Shabbat before *Purim*. The *Talmud* says that in the story of *Purim*, Haman, prime minister to King Achashverosh of Persia, casts lots to establish the best possible time to bring darkness into the world by wiping out the Israelites in Shushan. The lottery indicates that the annihilation should take place on the seventh day of the month of *Adar*, or Pisces. Knowing that Moses left the world on that day, Haman is happy, thinking this is an auspicious sign.

However, the commentators in the *Talmud* point out that Moses was also born on the seventh day of *Adar*. Like most truly righteous souls, Moses departed this world on the same day he entered it. This means that the month of *Adar* is also a time for miracles. The kabbalists explain that Haman was aware that both the potential for darkness and the opportunity to awaken the positive consciousness of Moses existed in the month of *Adar*. However, Haman believed that the death of Moses was the more powerful of the two forces—that it represented an exile of consciousness for the Israelites as well as the awakening of doubt in the minds of the people.

The Shabbat of Tetzaveh guides us in a choice between *Purim* consciousness and Amalek, doubting, consciousness. *Purim*, the cosmic window for the removal of uncertainty from our lives, and Amalek are polar opposites. Will we connect to the birth of Moses and the Light of the Creator, or will we allow Amalek to awaken, full of doubt and darkness? These are the choices available to us on the Shabbat of Tetzaveh as we prepare for *Purim*. This is why, when we read the additional section of Zachor at the end of the Torah reading of Tetzaveh, we receive special assistance in the form of a spark from the soul of Moses.

The portion of Tetzaveh begins with the Creator telling Moses, "*Ve'ata tetzaveh et benei Yisrael*," "And you shall command the Israelites." The word *tetzaveh* usually means "command," however, the *Zohar* explains that in this context, it means "a giving of support." So here the Creator is saying to Moses, "You shall come and be a part of them and give them support." On the Shabbat of Tetzaveh, the Creator is asking Moses to come and help us choose *Purim* consciousness over the darkness of Amalek. This is the only Shabbat of the year when Moses comes with a gift for each of us—whether we have earned it or not. He gives this spark of his soul to anyone who is open to it, allowing us to replace the negative power of doubt with true clarity.

Tetzaveh is also the only biblical portion since the birth of Moses where he is referred to indirectly but never mentioned by name. Why would this be so, especially in a portion where Moses figures so prominently? To help us understand this, Rabbi Jacob ben Asher, the *Baal HaTurim*, reminds us that after the Israelites committed the sin of the golden calf, the Creator came to Moses and said, "I will destroy all of them, and with you, Moses, I will create a whole new path." But Moses refused to go along, saying, "No. If You do not forgive them, I will have no part of Your plans. You can even erase me from Your Book." The kabbalists tell us that in response to this challenge, the Creator had to erase Moses from one of the portions of the Bible, and Tetzaveh is that portion.

But Moses' willingness to deny the Creator revealed tremendous Light, for not only was Moses taking upon himself the responsibility for many others, but he was willing to sacrifice his life for them. So as Rav Ashlag explains, another reason why the name of Moses is not mentioned on the Shabbat of Tetzaveh is because Moses' actions were so selfless that he no longer existed as an entity separate from the Creator. Where the name "Moses" is mentioned, a distinction is being drawn between the Creator and Moses, but on this Shabbat, we connect to complete *devekut*—to the complete unification of the soul of Moses with the Light of the Creator.

On the Shabbat of Tetzaveh, Moses opens up the gates so we can experience ultimate fulfillment. And he shows us the two things we must do to connect to this unending fulfillment during the rest of the year: We must awaken a desire to accept greater responsibility, and we must make any sacrifice necessary to live up to that responsibility.

KI TISA

The sages teach that when we read from the Torah, we awaken for the world the specific Light inherent in its passages. Most of the biblical portions we read during Shabbat contain uplifting events, but on the Shabbat of Ki Tisa, we read about the destruction caused by the sin of the golden calf. The obvious question, then, is what is the spiritual objective of Ki Tisa? What type of energy are we awakening for the world when we read about the golden calf?

Rav Isaac Luria, the Ari, says that we should not utter the names of certain angels at night, because by doing so, we call those angels to us. For much the same reason, we don't study things that relate to judgment if we are trying to remove judgment from our lives. So why do we study the sin of the Israelites and the golden calf if we don't want to bring negative energy into our lives? The portion of Ki Tisa contains a surprising lesson in this regard.

The *Talmud* says that while Moses was with the Creator on Mount Sinai, the Israelites fell spiritually by creating the idol of the golden calf. They did so at precisely the same moment that the Creator was handing over the first set of Tablets to Moses. This prompted the Creator to grab the Tablets back from Moses, but Moses held them tightly. The *Talmud* tells us that not only did Moses cling to the Tablets, but because of the enormous strength in his hands, Moses actually succeeded in wresting the Tablets away from the Creator.

We could endlessly explore this fascinating portion, but one of its many gifts is the lesson of *azut dekedushah*, or "holy audacity," which teaches us that we are not supposed to accept any decree as final, even when it comes from the Creator. We saw this lesson in the portion of Noah, when the Creator conveyed the message to King Hezekiah that he was going to die, and the king refused to accept the Creator's judgment. The sages tell us that the stories written in the *Talmud* are direct revelations from the Creator. The Creator, not Moses, is telling us this particular story about the golden calf because of the importance of the lesson here. "I do not accept this" has to become a constant part of our spiritual work; we also need to learn when to awaken this consciousness, and when not to.

One of my favorite kabbalists, Rabbi Avraham Yehoshua Heshil, also known as the *Ohev Yisrael*, or the Apte Rebbe, is famous for turning negative stories inside out and revealing the positive teaching within. Through his eyes, we see how extraordinary it is that at exactly the same moment the Creator was giving Moses the Tablets (the *Gemar HaTikkun*) on Mount Sinai, the sin of the golden calf was taking place at the foot of the mountain. This tells us that there is something unusually important about the sin of the golden calf.

The *Ohev Yisrael* says that Moses pulled the Tablets away from the Creator and descended from Mount Sinai, but when he saw the Israelites dancing around the golden calf, he threw the Tablets down and broke them. Why would he do this? Only a few minutes earlier, Moses had been struggling with the Creator to save the Tablets, knowing that the sin of the golden calf was taking place. But when Moses came down the mountain and actually saw the Israelites dancing around their newly created idol, he shattered the same Tablets he had fought so desperately to save. What meaning can we find in this seemingly contradictory behavior?

When people fall spiritually but acknowledge the error of their ways, there is always hope. However, if a person falls but continues to think he or she has done the correct thing, there is no opportunity for Light. When Moses descended the mountain, he was hoping the Israelites might have acknowledged their mistake in building the golden calf, but when he arrived at the encampment, he saw for himself that they had not. At that moment, Moses realized that the Israelites, in their present spiritual state, could not handle the Light of the *Gemar HaTikkun* from that first set of Tablets, so he let them fall from his hands.

We find this same insight about the value of acknowledging mistakes in a story about one of the students of the Baal Shem Tov. When the student arrived at a small town, weary and dusty from his long travels, the townsfolk gathered, each inviting him to stay in his home. After the student had chosen a place to spend the night, the wealthiest man in the town complained, "How can you stay at this person's house? We all know he has done terrible things, whereas everyone in town can vouch for me, plus I can provide you with far more comfortable lodgings."

The student of the Baal Shem Tov replied, "When a person falls, no matter how low, the Creator is always with him. But if a person is full of pride, the Creator cannot abide by him. You are correct in saying this man is responsible for many negative deeds. But the Creator is still with him. You, on the other hand, are so proud of your goodness that the Creator is not at your side, and if the Creator cannot stay with you, neither can I."

When we read the story of Adam and the Tree of Knowledge of Good and Evil, Adam seems to choose to eat from the Tree of Knowledge of Good and Evil. But according to the *Midrash*, in truth he had no choice. The sin of Adam, as it is called, was inevitable—and for the best. If Adam had not fallen and had instead achieved the *Gemar HaTikkun* in the Garden of Eden, it would not have lasted long. The Final Correction has to be earned. So although it seems as if what Adam did was negative, it was not. The spiritual fall of Adam made possible the emergence of our world from darkness and made clear what we have to accomplish to bring about the *Gemar HaTikkun.*

The *Talmud* explains that the same is true of the Israelites waiting for Moses at the foot of Mount Sinai. They, too, had no choice when they built the golden calf. That first set of Tablets was never meant to come down intact into this world. If it had, and had the Israelites received it, the Light revealed would have been very unstable. This is why the Creator came to Moses after he broke the Tablets and said, in effect, "Don't berate yourself. In truth, you've done a good thing, for now I can give you something even better. Not only will this second set of Tablets include the Ten Utterances, it will also contain the *Midrash* and all the laws."

If we want to extricate a diamond embedded in glass, we will need to break the glass to remove it. When Moses brought down the first set of Tablets and broke them, he was actually revealing the Light they contained. On the Shabbat of Ki Tisa, we awaken to the understanding that there was no negativity in the sin of the golden calf. Not only were the Israelites not the evildoers we imagine, but they were making a great sacrifice for the rest of us. They were willing to take upon themselves the condemnation of history. Ki Tisa is a positive story—a story of Light—and now that we understand its message, we can never read the story of the sin of the golden calf the same way again.

Rabbi Zadok HaKohen Rabinowitz, the *Pri Tzadik*, says that at the moment of the Final Correction, the *Gemar HaTikkun*, we are going to look back at all the terrible mistakes we made and realize how perfect they really were. The *Gemar HaTikkun* is not the moment when all the corrections will be made; it is the time when we come to the realization that all the mistakes we made were perfect, that all our failings were blessings, and that all those dark places we found ourselves in were truly filled with Light.

VAYAK'HEL

This biblical portion begins with the words *"Vayek'hel Moshe,"* "And Moses gathered." Moses often gathered the Israelites together during their time in the desert, but the words used to describe this particular gathering indicate that something special was taking place. According to the kabbalists, during the forty-nine days between leaving Egypt (*Pesach*) and receiving the Torah at Mount Sinai (*Shavuot*), the Israelites made enormous efforts to strengthen their Desire to Share. They awakened love and unity within themselves and accepted responsibility for sharing it with the world. This Desire to Share was the seed of the Revelation at Mount Sinai, the catalyst for *bila hamavet lanetzach*, the gift of immortality that was given to the Israelites before the creation of the golden calf.

In *Ten Luminous Emanations*, Rav Ashlag says it is impossible for us to connect to the ultimate level of *bila hamavet lanetzach*—the end of pain, suffering, and death in our world—without being one with every other person in this world. In fact, we must be one, not just with all living things but with the entire inanimate world as well. Unity is the true revelation at Mount Sinai.

In this context, what is sin? Sin is separation. Rabbi Yehuda Loew, the Maharal of Prague, explains that in Genesis, as the one river flows out of the Garden of Eden, it divides into four smaller rivers. The Maharal says that the negative side was created at the place where the river divided, where it ceased to be one. When it comes down to it, there are only two forces in this world: Unity and separation. Ultimate unity is *bila hamavet lanetzach*, or immortality; ultimate separation is death. When Moses gathered the Israelites in the desert, he awakened and strengthened their connection to themselves and to others. The gift of the Shabbat of Vayek'hel is to awaken the power of unity.

The Shabbat of Vayek'hel also brings us the clarity to realize that just because we help another person doesn't mean that we are unified with that person. When a dentist takes care of a toothache, does this mean the dentist is unified with his patient? We have to be careful not to delude ourselves into thinking that just because we do good things for others, we are unified with them or we are awakening love between us and them. We need to acknowledge the very real difference, and its importance, for to the degree that we are separate from others, we are separated from the Creator.

The only way we can receive the awesome gift of unity on the Shabbat of Vayak'hel is to work at it and to keep our eyes on the prize. Am I more open to others today than I was yesterday? Do I have more love for them this week than last week? Do I care more for you this month than I did last month? Such questions keep us focused on our all-important goal.

In a lovely passage in the *Shacharit*, the morning prayers, we see that when the angels prepare to open up the channels to reveal Light to this world, they give permission to one another with love. The angels know that one cannot bring Light into this world without first awakening love. When we help another person, part of our spiritual work is to ask for assistance from the Creator to truly love this other person, to truly care for him or her. When we understand that we need this opening to truly love and care—and we ask for it—the Creator will give it to us.

The *Zohar* says that if true unity existed among just ten people, *Mashiach*, the Messiah, would come and pain, suffering, and death would be removed from our world. But set aside the number ten for a moment. If you and one other person were able to truly achieve unity, imagine how much Light this would reveal for you—and for all of us. This is one-fifth of the requirement for *Mashiach*, right?

Unity is *Mashiach*. Separation is death. The power of unity is the great gift Moses is willing to give us on the Shabbat of Vayak'hel, once we make the necessary preparations.

PEKUDEI

In the portion of Pekudei, the Israelites collect all the gold, silver, fabric, and wood necessary for the construction of the Tabernacle, which Moses then builds. This sounds very straightforward, but when we read the *Midrash*, we realize that what actually took place, particularly the back-story, was much more complicated.

Moses had descended from Mount Sinai with the second set of Tablets, returning to the Israelites with a message from the Creator: They were to build a Tabernacle where the Light of the Creator would dwell. So for the next month or so, the Israelites gathered the requisite building materials. And what happened once all the wood and gold and silver and fabric had been collected in accordance with the Creator's specifications? Absolutely nothing. The *Midrash* says that all the materials were packed away in a corner somewhere as days turned into weeks, which turned into months. To make matters worse, a group of Israelites took it upon themselves to complain tirelessly to Moses and to grumble about his leadership to anyone who would listen.

But Moses never lost his composure. He remained silent in the face of all the complaining and criticism. Can you imagine not reacting to months of grumbling and popular discontent? Moses remained above the fray, for unlike the rest of us, he had no need, or even desire, for anyone's approval. Moses simply left everything that had been gathered for the Tabernacle untouched, waiting for the Creator's instructions. And when those instructions did not come right away, Moses did nothing.

Moses did not let a need for approval distract him from what really mattered—and neither can we. With the example of Moses to guide us, we can seek the inner strength to stay the course and not give in to the temptations of popular approval. And when we succeed in our efforts, our connection to the Light of the Creator strengthens.

Once there was a man in Poland who was so ill that his doctors had given up any hope for him. So he went to see Rabbi Israel Meir Kagan, the *Chofetz Chaim*, and asked the great sage to pray for his recovery. The *Chofetz Chaim* replied, "I am sorry. I cannot help you, but there is a man in another village who may be able to do so. I will give you his name, but on one condition: You must promise never to tell anyone else about him."

The sick man agreed and followed the Rabbi's directions to a modest house in a nearby village. The healer was a humble man, who accommodated the sick man's request for a blessing and sent him on his way. After returning home, the sick man prepared himself for death, but to his surprise, he grew a little stronger each day until finally he was fully recovered. It was a miracle, he told his wife, but in keeping with his promise to the *Chofetz Chaim*, he refused to give her any but the scantiest details.

Thirty years passed, and the sister-in-law of the man who had been miraculously cured fell ill with cancer. The man's wife came to him and said, "My sister is very sick. Please tell her where you went all those years ago when you were miraculously healed, so she can go, too." The man replied, "I'm sorry, but I swore to the *Chofetz Chaim* that I would never reveal the name of the man who healed me." But his wife, who loved her sister dearly, kept prodding and pushing until finally her husband gave in.

So the two sisters retraced the man's steps to the village. Thankfully, the man who had given the blessing was still alive and happy to oblige the sister-in-law with a blessing, too. But this time, nothing happened. The blessing had no effect. So the wife begged her husband to go back to the *Chofetz Chaim*, for perhaps he could recommend someone else with the power to heal her sister. When her husband went to the *Chofetz Chaim* and told him the whole story, the *Chofetz Chaim* replied, "Thirty years ago, I was much younger and I was able to fast and perform the prayers necessary to heal you, but now they are beyond me."

As the sage's words sunk in, the man realized it was not the stranger in the nearby village who had healed him all those years ago, but the *Chofetz Chaim* himself with his fasting and prayers. Because the *Chofetz Chaim* had not wanted any recognition for his good deeds, he had sent the sick man to a random person in the village nearby for a blessing. The *Chofetz Chaim* knew that if the truth got out, he would become famous for his healing powers and would run the risk not only of becoming fond of his reputation, but of polishing it by seeking the approval of others.

When we seek approval, we are all too likely to lose our connection to the Light of the Creator, which is, ironically, the source of all our talents. Approval can be dangerously seductive to even the most spiritually elevated among us. But when we can resist its temptations, our ability to help others grows ever stronger.

LEVITICUS

VAYIKRA

In the previous portion of Pekudei, Moses completes the construction of the Tabernacle as the Creator commanded him. This portion begins with the words *"Vayikra El Moshe,"* "The Creator calls to Moses." According to the kabbalists, the Torah was created when the Creator asked Moses to inscribe it according to the Creator's wishes. But when they reached the portion of Vayikra, the Creator and Moses had a difference of opinion over how to proceed. Rabbi Jacob ben Asher, the *Baal HaTurim*, says that the Creator told Moses to write the first word of the portion as *vayikra*, which includes the letter *Alef*, so that Moses could let everyone know how closely connected he was to the Creator. (The greater the *Alef*, the greater the *ani*, or "me.")

But Moses replied that he would prefer to write it a little differently. Moses wanted to leave out the letter *Alef* and write the word as *veyikar* ("And He happened upon"). This would make it seem as if the Creator spoke to Moses only in dreams, or inadvertently, or as a matter of coincidence. But the Creator told Moses he could not use the word *veyikar*; the letter *Alef* had to be included.

Moses eventually agreed, but only on the condition that the Creator let him write the *Alef* smaller than the other letters, thereby diminishing the appearance of his connection with the Creator. In fact, the *Alef* is so small that when we look at the word *vayikra* in the Torah from a distance, we see it as *veyikar*.

How many of us would respond as Moses did? If it were you or I instead of Moses, we might have asked to make the *Alef* larger than all the other letters! But Moses knew, as did the *Chofetz Chaim* in our exploration of the previous portion, that the best way to maintain a constant connection to the Light of the Creator is by keeping it private, far from the possibility of approval or disapproval from other people.

In the desert, the Israelites judged Moses harshly because they doubted his connection to the Creator, so the temptation to reveal how close that relationship truly was must have been very strong for Moses. Nevertheless, Moses fought with the Creator to minimize any public acknowledgment of his special status. Moses shows us that the smaller our *Alef*, the less obvious our level of connection to the Light of the Creator is to others and the stronger our *vayikra*—our constant connection to the Light of the Creator—becomes.

Rabbi Shlomo Yitzchaki, or Rashi, the great scholar known for his comprehensive commentary on the Bible, says that when Moses stood in front of the newly completed Tabernacle, surrounded by thousands of people, the Creator called to him. Rashi asks, "Why and how did this call go out to Moses?" and then answers his own question. "The Voice came to Moses, and no one else heard it." Rashi makes it clear that this Call of the Creator was not a whisper—it was so loud and powerful that it could snap trees. It was so loud that Moses became frightened, yet no one else could hear it! The Shabbat of Vayikra gives us the opportunity to be the *Vayikra El Moshe*, the one who hears the Calling of the Creator. But we cannot have both that connection and the public recognition of our privileged position. If we are going to be truly connected to the Light of the Creator, the Calling of the Creator can be for our ears alone.

The *Zohar* says, "How we see our lives is exactly how our lives will be." Every day, dozens of things that happen, large and small, may please or upset us. How do we evaluate their significance? How we choose to perceive the little things—those moments we could view as messages or coincidences or annoyances—either pushes away the Light of the Creator or draws the Light of the Creator into our life. Keeping this firmly in mind, I chose to see my occupied bathroom as *vayikra*, another message from the Creator alerting me to an opportunity to practice patience and to diminish my ego!

TZAV

Usually when something spiritually important happens on a particular date, we celebrate it on the anniversary of that same date, whether it falls on a Tuesday or a Wednesday or any other day. This is not true of the 10th day of *Nissan*, however. The Torah tells us that the first *Shabbat HaGadol*—the first revelation of the Light of Redemption—occurred on the 10th day of the month of *Nissan* on Shabbat, and this revelation of Light occurs again each year on the Shabbat preceding Passover, irrespective of whether the 10th of *Nissan* falls on Shabbat or not. And if that isn't a strong enough indication of the importance of the Shabbat of Tzav, it is the only Shabbat in the entire year that merits the name *Shabbat HaGadol*, or "the Great Shabbat."

There are various explanations for this Shabbat's prominence, all of which fall along similar lines. Rabbi Yitzchak Myer Alter, the *Chidushei HaRim*, says it's called the Great Shabbat because all the Lights revealed on all the other Shabbats of the year come together as one on this day. Rabbi Chaim ben Attar, the *Or HaChaim*, says we have a tremendous opportunity on the Shabbat of Tzav to open the Gates of Redemption with the assistance of the accumulated Light available for us. Other kabbalistic sages affirm that the Redemption from Egypt occurred in the month of *Nissan* and that the *Gemar HaTikkun*, the Final Correction, will also occur in this month.

The 10th day of *Nissan* is also the date on which Rav Ashlag's teacher, whose name has never been revealed, left this world. Rav Shimon bar Yochai completed the revelation of the *Zohar* in the world, but all the Light of the *Zohar* was stuck in the Upper Worlds. Even the work of the Ari and the Baal Shem Tov was not enough to bring the Light of the *Zohar* down to us. It was Rav Ashlag's teacher who opened the gate for Rav Ashlag to be able to truly bring this Light of Wisdom to the world. As we saw in the portion of Yitro, the soul of a righteous person is like a father to other souls, and its Light is particularly accessible to others on the righteous person's birth and death dates. Since Rav Ashlag's teacher made possible the extraordinary work of Rav Ashlag—including his *Sulam* commentary on the *Zohar*; his *Talmud Eser Sefirot*, considered the central textbook for students of Kabbalah; and his tireless devotion to spreading the wisdom of Kabbalah throughout the world—there is no greater day in the year to connect to the source of this wisdom than the 10th of *Nissan*.

I would like to share with you a letter Rav Ashlag wrote to his uncle, explaining his spiritual process with his teacher. In this letter, Rav Ashlag gives us access to a great fount of Light from his teacher, which is available to us even more on the Shabbat of Tzav, the Great Shabbat. Rav Ashlag writes: "On Friday, the 12th day of *Cheshvan*, a man came to me. In talking to him, I realized that he was a great and wise man, and not only was he wise in Kabbalah, but he also had tremendous knowledge of other wisdoms as well."

It is interesting to note that those who are able to truly open up the Gates of Wisdom are often people who are willing and able to draw from many sources. For example, Rav Kook, the Chief Rabbi of Palestine during the time of Rav Ashlag, was a kabbalist, but he was also a student of art. Rav Kook believed that Rembrandt was a *tzadik*, a righteous person, who received the inspiration for his paintings from the *Or HaGanuz*, the Light concealed by the Creator at the time of the Creation. Rav Kook's knowledge and appreciation of art helped him open up the gates of the wisdom of Kabbalah to the world, just as the other wisdoms of Rav Ashlag's teacher and of Rav Ashlag would help them.

Rav Ashlag continues with his letter to his uncle: "In the first meeting with my teacher, I had already begun to taste great wisdom from him." In the Introduction to *Talmud Eser Sefirot* (*Ten Luminous Emanations*), Rav Ashlag explains that the purpose of our spiritual work is not merely intellectual, but sensual; one of the highest achievements is to actually have a physical sense, a physical taste, of the Light of the Creator in everything around us.

In his letter, Rav Ashlag goes on to say: "As I was talking to this man, it became clear to me that he had a huge ego...." What does this observation reveal? In the relationship between teacher and student, there will always be an opening for judgment. We find this with Rav Isaac Luria, the Ari, and his student, Rav Chaim Vital; with the Baal Shem Tov and his student, the Magid of Mezritch; with Rav Ashlag and his teacher; and with my father, the Rav, and his teacher, Rav Brandwein. Wherever there is an opportunity for great Light, there will also be an opportunity to misjudge the situation—to see it as exactly the opposite of what it truly is. If you and I met someone like Rav Ashlag's teacher—someone with enormous wisdom who seemed to us to also have a big ego—we would have a decision to make. Is learning from him an opportunity we should pursue? Or should we let it pass because of what we judge to be this person's flaws? We are often so quick to judge that we can never know what gates we are closing, but fortunately, Rav Ashlag did not fall prey to this mistake.

Rav Ashlag goes on: "I felt there was something deeper here; I believed in this man. And he promised to reveal to me all the wisdom of Kabbalah. Every night for three months, I went to his house after midnight and I studied with him." Rav Ashlag was hoping that his teacher would reveal to him the secrets of our universe and how the worlds came into being, but it turned out that his teacher didn't want to teach him such things. He wanted to focus solely on Rav Ashlag's personal qualities.

Once again, Rav Ashlag was faced with an opportunity for judgment. Every night for three months, he went to his teacher, believing that his teacher would reveal great secrets to him. But instead of unraveling great mysteries, his teacher would tell Rav Ashlag what he needed to change in order to become more pure. This was certainly *not* what Rav Ashlag was hoping for, but it taught him, and us, a great lesson—that knowing what we need to change in ourselves is the only true purpose of study. If we think that study is limited to pondering the wisdom of the sages, then we are not achieving the real objective of this work. Rav Ashlag's teacher kept telling him that as long as we strive to uncover and minimize this immense ego we all possess, we are growing spiritually. Forget about anything else.

Rav Ashlag writes: "Of course, I kept on pushing him to teach me at least one secret, and every once in a while, my teacher would begin revealing a secret to me, but he would never finish. He never gave me the feeling of having had a complete secret revealed to me; he never gave me the satisfaction of knowing one thing completely."

Here we learn another valuable lesson: The hallmark of true spiritual work comes when the teaching is over and we are left with an even greater desire to learn, to grow, and to change. If we are sated by what we're learning, we have lost our way. Knowing this, Rav Ashlag's teacher made sure that Rav Ashlag was left with a sense of yearning at the end of every study session, carefully limiting the scope of every revelation.

Rav Ashlag continues: "Once I pushed him and pushed him and pushed him until he finally revealed to me one complete secret. I felt such great joy and total satisfaction with this great wisdom that he revealed to me. But after that great revelation, my ego began growing, and when that happened, my teacher began pulling away from me."

Rav Ashlag sensed this loss only in hindsight. What did he feel at the time? Nothing. In his words: "I couldn't tell that my teacher was becoming distant from me." Such is the power of self-satisfaction. At this point in his life, Rav Ashlag was already a tremendous kabbalist. He had been studying Kabbalah since age seven, and for three months, he had been working day and night with his new teacher to remove his ego and to purify himself, and still he was completely blind to the chasm that was opening between himself and his teacher.

If there is ever a moment in our life when we think we have achieved clarity, when we congratulate ourselves for our ability to truly see, we just have to stop for a second and think about Rav Ashlag. If this great kabbalist was so blinded by his ego, how can we possibly think that we ourselves are not likely to be clueless?

"For three months, there was a growing divide between me and my teacher, but I did not feel it. Toward the end of these three months, I couldn't even physically find him. I would go to his house, and he would not be there. I would look for him to no avail. Then, and only then, did I begin sensing that he had truly removed himself from me. And then, finally, my pain drove me to work on my ego and my selfishness."

Rav Ashlag went through a process of purification that evidently met with success. "On the 9th day of *Nissan* in the morning, I found my teacher and begged him to take me back as a student, which he did. Now, for the second time, he revealed to me a great complete secret, this time concerning a *mikveh* [ritual bath]. And of course, I was tremendously happy. That day, I noticed that he was becoming weak, however, so I did not leave his house. The next day, on the 10th day of *Nissan*, his soul left this world. May his merit protect us."

There were only two times during Rav Ashlag's relationship with his teacher that Rav Ashlag felt satisfaction. The first was when he pushed his teacher to reveal one great secret, which led to his teacher becoming distant. The second was when he received a second complete secret from his teacher, just before his teacher died. Rav Ashlag writes: "I cannot express in words the tremendous pain I felt. My hope was that my teacher was going to reveal to me wisdom and elevate me to a level of one of the great souls that ever lived. But I was left with nothing. Not only did I lose all hope of ever gaining more wisdom, but the pain of his passing was so great that I also lost all the wisdom that my teacher had ever taught me."

Rav Ashlag lost all hope of ever gaining more wisdom, or of even finding the wisdom he had lost, but in time, his despair gave way to a new feeling. As he put it: "From that moment on, I looked up to Heaven and I awakened a tremendous amount of yearning. Not for one moment in the day did I set aside this yearning, this work, until I, through the merit of my teacher and his wisdom, achieved a certain level of merit in the eyes of the Creator. At that moment, the Gates of Wisdom, the flow of this Well of Wisdom, was awakened within me, and I was reminded, through the assistance of the Creator, of all the secrets that my teacher had revealed to me. I thank the Creator for keeping me alive and giving me the merit to receive this wisdom."

Here we learn another precious lesson from Rav Ashlag: Any great revelation is preceded by a time of terrible darkness. Hopelessness comes before a time of great elevation. This is the reality of spiritual growth. Rav Ashlag ends his letter by saying: "How can I even thank the Creator? The Creator knew all along how little I had, that I didn't have understanding, I didn't even have enough Light and wisdom to give thanks for the great gifts I had received, and certainly not enough to deserve them. But the Creator chooses whomever He chooses to reveal His Light."

Rav Ashlag had reached a spiritual level so elevated that he no longer believed that he had earned—or deserved—anything at all. The great Light that he was able to channel no longer had anything to do with who *he* was.

There are many important teachings on the Shabbat of Tzav, but I am particularly taken with the tremendous opportunity we have on the 10th of *Nissan*, on *Shabbat HaGadol*, to bind ourselves to the great soul of Rav Ashlag's teacher. And through this connection, we may also achieve a measure of *devekut*, or unification with the soul of Rav Ashlag, and open up the Gates of Wisdom, regardless of what we deserve.

SHEMINI

The word *shemini* means "eighth." The Torah passage of Shemini begins with: "And it came to pass on the eighth day that Moses called Aaron and his sons and the elders of Israel…." Once the physical structure of the Tabernacle was complete, Moses worked alone inside it for an additional eight days before gathering the elders. Since we know that everything in the Torah has meaning beyond the literal, what is the significance of the time Moses spent alone in the Tabernacle? Why eight days?

In *Chesed Le Avraham*, Kabbalist Rabbi Avraham Azulai says: "When the world was created, there was also a creation of 50 Gates of Purity and elevation, which are controlled by the angel Michael and all of the angels that support him. So, too, were 50 Gates of Impurity and darkness created, which are controlled by the most negative of angels, the *Samech-Mem*." Kabbalah teaches us that there is always a balance in the world between positive and negative, good and evil, Light and darkness. We see that balance present in the two pathways

Rabbi Azulai describes for our souls to travel: They can either elevate through the 50 Gates of Purity or descend through the 50 Gates of Darkness.

Rabbi David Shlomo Eibshitz, the *Arvei Nachal*, explains that when we connect, grow, and transform spiritually for eight consecutive days, we complete the process necessary to elevate into the gate above the one we are currently in. So if we begin at the beginning of the system that the *Arvei Nachal* describes and we're able to stay unswervingly on track spiritually for 400 days in a row, then by the end of the last day, we will have completed our elevation to the highest gate, the 50th Gate of Purity. Conversely, if we begin at the beginning and manage to be completely disconnected from the Light of the Creator for 400 days in a row, on the 400th day, we will pass through the lowest gate—the 50th Gate of Impurity. According to the *Zohar*, Moses entered into the 50th Gate of Purity, and "on the eighth day" refers to the energy and power needed to push each one of us through one of the 50 gates.

The *Zohar* and the Ari tell us that before the Israelites left Egypt, they were at the 49th Gate of Impurity, which meant they were in grave spiritual danger of falling to the very bottom. The miracle of Passover is that even though the Israelites had not earned elevation out of the 49th Gate of Impurity, the Creator infused them with a tremendous amount of Light. Then the Israelites spent the next 49 days between Passover and *Shavuot* working successfully to rise out of the Gates of Impurity altogether. Today, these 49 days are known as the Counting of the Omer.

The *Arvei Nachal* explains that the Counting of the Omer unleashes miraculous power. It accelerates our progress through space and time so that when we connect with this spiritual tool, we fly through an entire gate—eight days' worth of nonstop spiritual work—in just a few minutes. By counting the Omer for just five to ten minutes every night during the 49 days between Passover and *Shavuot*, we are, in effect, able to do the work of 400 days!

Why did the Creator give us access to this fantastic force? For one thing, He wanted to give the Israelites a vehicle for climbing out of the deep spiritual hole they were in before they left Egypt. Also, the *Chesed Le Avraham* tells us, the Creator realized there was a flaw in the dynamics of Creation that could allow a soul to enter into the 50th Gate of Impurity and never be able to get out. So the Creator created the Counting of the Omer, a system whereby everyone would always have an opportunity to keep themselves from falling into the 50th Gate of Impurity. By making the Counting of the Omer available to us every year at the time of Passover, we can always stop our spiritual fall and swiftly climb out of any darkness we may have tumbled into.

As Rabbi Avraham Azulai says, "We count for 49 days and on the 50th day—*Shavuot*—there is the revelation called the Torah, the revelation of freedom from death. At *Shavuot*, everyone should have achieved a level of connection, of purity, of holiness, according to their spiritual growth. Even the lowest possible soul in the world, who is at the 49th Gate of Impurity at the beginning of the Counting of the Omer but who makes that connection, will begin to taste the Light of the Creator by the time *Shavuot* comes around, since he will have risen to the first of the 50 Gates of Purity. And whoever has already elevated out of the Gates of Impurity and connects to the Counting of the Omer can enter the 50th Gate of Purity at *Shavuot* and achieve freedom from the Angel of Death."

On the Shabbat of Shemini, Moses gives each of us the opportunity to enjoy an amazing spiritual boost by connecting to the accelerated spiritual process of the 49 days of the Counting of the Omer.

The biblical story of Shemini tells us that Aaron joined Moses after Moses had worked alone for eight days in the Tabernacle. Then Aaron, along with his sons, Nadav and Avihu, helped Moses with the complex work of setting up the Tabernacle and preparing the prescribed sacrifices and incense. Rashi tells us that when everything was done and the Israelites were gathered before the Tabernacle, the Light of the Creator, the *Shechinah*, still had not come to rest on the Tabernacle. At that moment, Aaron realized that he was responsible for this failure. By taking part in the creation of the golden calf, he could not be a channel for the Light to the Creator. He was blocking the Light. Immediately, Moses took Aaron into the Tabernacle and, together, they begged for the Light of the Creator to come down and rest on their work.

Rabbi Menachem Mendel Morgensztern of Kotzk, the Kotzker Rebbe, said that when our soul descends into this world, it comes down a ladder, and as we are born, we fall off this ladder. He explains that our process in life is to jump toward the ladder again and grab onto it. There are some people who jump ten times and then stop jumping. There are some people who jump a hundred times and then stop jumping. And then there are those unique and special souls who keep jumping, no matter what. When you keep jumping, no matter what, eventually the Creator elevates you back up onto that ladder.

We all know that at some point in our spiritual process, we will go through a difficult time. As we saw with Rav Ashlag in the portion of Tzav, the most challenging moments usually come just before the most dramatic revelations. Still, it seems somehow unjust when the moment comes to reveal the Light that we've worked so hard for and nothing happens. But what happens at that point depends on us. The choice is always ours. We can decide to give up, or we can follow the example of Moses and Aaron. On the Shabbat of Shemini, they give us the strength to continue, to give it one more try with the Creator.

One good reason not to give up is the possibility that we may come to see things in an entirely new way, especially when it looks as if the worst has befallen us. Once we understand what has truly happened, we may gain a revelatory new insight into how life works. The Bible says that after the Light of the Creator, the *Shechinah*, came to rest on the Tabernacle, the two sons of Aaron, Nadav and Avihu, entered the Tabernacle and died. They left this world. The Bible continues: "...and Aaron was silent." The kabbalists go further, saying that not only was Aaron silent, he was full of joy. How could this be?

The only reason we ever feel pain is because we do not see the bigger picture of what is going on in our lives; we do not have the perspective of Aaron. The *Zohar* explains that Aaron's sons, Nadav and Avihu, were two of the greatest souls of their generation. On this eighth day, when the world was enjoying one of the greatest spiritual peaks in history, it was revealed to Nadav and Avihu that they had a choice: They could either live out the rest of their days in this world or they could prepare their souls for even more important work.

The *Zohar* says that after Nadav and Avihu made their choice and their two souls left the world, they rose higher and higher. They elevated to such heights that they joined with the soul of Pinchas and returned to Earth where they became the soul of Elijah the Prophet. If we could see this, as Aaron did, we would realize that there is no reason to grieve in the face of death. We may feel the loss of connection, but Aaron was able to see the souls of Nadav and Avihu so clearly that he never disconnected from them, not even for one second. He saw their souls becoming the Light of Elijah.

Rabbi Moshe Chaim Luzzatto, the Ramchal explains that life is like a great maze made of tall hedges. For someone who has the vision of Aaron—the ability to see the deeper truth of things—it's as if he or she were looking down on the maze from a tall tree. From there, this person can clearly see the path in and out. However, when we are inside the maze, it is all too easy to get lost or stuck. We must truly grow our desire to achieve this elevated clarity of vision because if we don't, life will be painful, full of fear and darkness. But the good news is that when we push ourselves toward attaining this higher totality of vision, we can achieve it. We can reach the point where there is no sadness, but only the greatest elevation of joy.

The portion of Shemini teaches us the value of learning about the amazing spiritual tools at our disposal and then using them. It teaches us the importance of persevering, especially when things look desperate, for the darkest hour is always just before the dawn. And it teaches us the limitless joy that can be ours when we raise our sights, as Aaron did, to find that what could be the most terribly painful moments in life are actually opportunities to see the larger truth, to elevate beyond the power of death.

TAZRIA-METZORA

Except in leap years in the kabbalistic calendar, the Torah portion of Tazria is read together with the portion of Metzora on the same Shabbat. The word *tazria* means "she conceived," which refers to the laws of purification after childbirth, and *metzora* means "leper," which refers to the complicated rituals for cleansing a leper and the home of a leper. We become awakened on this Shabbat to seize every opportunity to speak positively and to assist others.

A long time ago, the *Talmud* tells us, there was a merchant who traveled from city to city and from town to town, selling what he claimed was a miracle that could transform anyone's life. When the great sage Rav Yannai heard about this merchant and his self-proclaimed miracle, he sent a servant to invite the man to his house. When the merchant was told that Rav Yannai wanted to see him, he replied that what he was selling was not for people like Rav Yannai. The messenger insisted, telling the merchant in no uncertain terms that he should accompany him to Rav Yannai's home.

At the door, Rav Yannai graciously welcomed the merchant, saying, "I hear you have a remedy that can transform people's lives. Would you be so kind as to share it with me?" The merchant paused a few moments for dramatic effect. Then he reached into his worn rucksack, opened up the Book of Psalms, and began to read aloud: "Who is the man who desires life and loves days that he may see good in them? Keep your tongue from evil and your lips from speaking negatively. Refrain from evil and do good; seek peace and pursue it." Then the merchant closed the book and smiled. "This is what I'm selling."

Rav Yannai clapped his hands and laughed aloud, his eyes sparkling with delight as he invited the merchant to join him for dinner. "I have read this verse many times," the sage remarked, "but not until this very moment have I realized how important its message is."

Why did Rav Yannai take such pleasure in the merchant's reading? The *Zohar* tells us that *lashon hara,* meaning "negative or evil speech," is the worst form of darkness. Its most obvious form is malicious gossip, but there are other kinds of *lashon hara.* We may talk about ourselves in negative ways, for example, or in a moment of anger, we may say hurtful things to others. If we were asked which is worse, walking up to a stranger in the street and slapping him in the face or speaking badly about someone else over dinner with a friend, most of us would say the former. King David, however, who wrote the Book of Psalms, would disagree. Why? What is so toxic about *lashon hara*?

To understand exactly why negative speech is so detrimental, we need to delve more deeply into its spiritual source. The seed of pain, suffering, and, ultimately, death was introduced into our world when the serpent spoke *lashon hara* about the Creator, first to Eve and then to Adam, in the Garden of Eden. The serpent told Eve that the Creator had instructed her not to eat from the Tree of Knowledge because the Creator did not want her to become as smart as He was. Because Adam and Eve listened to the words of the serpent, they fell spiritually.

Most negative actions we take can be set right through a process called *teshuvah*, or spiritual correction. After slapping that stranger across the face, for example, we can remove the darkness we have brought upon ourselves through a two-step process. The first step is physical: We ask the injured party for forgiveness. This opens the way for the second aspect of the correction: The spiritual Light that comes into our soul when we truly see our action for what it is and seek to make amends.

Lashon hara, however, was the original negative action—the seed that brought all the darkness that followed. When we use *lashon hara*, or negative speech, we reconnect to the power of the serpent and create a shell of negativity around our soul, which prevents any Light we draw through our spiritual work from entering. This is why the damage done by *lashon hara* cannot be healed by the process of *teshuvah*.

So the first gift we receive on the Shabbat of Tazria-Metzora is a renewed appreciation for the power of our words. We are now aware that speaking negatively blocks us from the Light, but if we hold back from assisting others—either through word or deed—this, too, cuts us off from the Light of the Creator.

One day, Rav Chiya and Rav Yosi, two students of Rav Shimon bar Yochai, were traveling when they came across a man whose face was ravaged by leprosy. They stopped to help the man, trying to discover what he had done to cause such a disconnection from the Light of the Creator. The man responded angrily, thinking they were making fun of him, and threatened them with a beating once his sons returned.

While the three men were talking, the man's sons arrived. But instead of taking up their father's cause, they saw what was really going on—that the souls of Rav Chiya and Rav Yosi had come to help their father. The youngest son said to Rav Chiya and Rav Yosi, "The reason our father has leprosy is because in the city where we live, there are many negative people committing all kinds of negative acts, but our father did not want to confront them. Not only did he not try to help them change their ways, but he also stopped us, his sons, when we wanted to do something to try to awaken them."

Once the leper realized that Rav Chiya and Rav Yosi were really trying to help him, he was very grateful. They responded by telling him that they were not helping him for his own sake. Rather, they were doing it to manifest Light within their own souls, and if they did not seize this opportunity that had presented itself, they would be diminished by their inaction, much the way he himself had been. When we know of someone whom we could help but choose not to, this may not seem like such a terrible thing. But by deciding not to speak or act on their behalf, we not only miss an opportunity to help, but we diminish the Light of our own souls.

One of the things that makes choosing not to help and *lashon hara*, negative or evil speech, so insidious is that words themselves seem like such small, unimportant things. While we do our best to avoid big negative actions, sometimes we permit ourselves small negative deeds. Rav Ashlag says we behave this way because, on some level, we don't view ourselves as being particularly important. We tell ourselves that if we were Moses or some other great soul, we would be very careful with all of our actions, both great and small. But because we think we are not Moses or Rav Shimon bar Yochai, we believe that the small stuff doesn't matter.

Rav Ashlag says that *how* we view ourselves determines *who* we are. The Creator has given us the choice to elevate ourselves by growing spiritually or to diminish ourselves by deciding that what we do doesn't really matter. When we participate in this Shabbat of Tazria-Metzora and come to hear the Torah reading, we reconnect with the knowledge that every word we say matters because we ourselves matter, not in an egotistical sense but because of our unlimited potential to reveal—or to suppress—great Light with every choice we make.

ACHAREI MOT-KEDOSHIM

The portions of Acharei Mot and Kedoshim are also generally read together, except when there is a leap year in the kabbalistic calendar. The Torah reading of Acharei Mot, which precedes the portion of Kedoshim, begins with the words: "The Creator spoke to Moses (*acharei mot*) of the two sons of Aaron [Nadav and Avihu], when they came close to the Creator and they died."

Rabbi Elimelech of Lizhensk, the *Noam Elimelech*, says that the words *acharei mot*, meaning "after the death," at the beginning of this portion do more than refer to the events that take place after the deaths of Nadav and Avihu, the sons of Aaron. He says these words mean that we have the power to be "after death," to transcend its power. He explains that this potential to leave death behind, to go past death, is the Light revealed on the Shabbat of Acharei Mot-Kedoshim.

There is a state that the *tzadikim*, or elevated souls, achieve, where the connection to the body is no longer selfish. When we reach this elevated state of consciousness, we gain complete dominion over the Angel of Death. He can no longer touch us. We can decide that we have completed our work here on Earth, and we can just let go. In the case of Nadav and Avihu, they still had more work to do, but they had become so enamored with their connection to the Light of the Creator that they decided to accelerate the process of their *devekut*, or complete union. They felt such love for the Creator's Light that they simply left their bodies behind.

According to the *Midrash Rabbah*, one of the most revered scholars of the first century CE, Rabbi Akiva, had a vast number of students, more than 24,000, one of whom was Rav Shimon bar Yochai, who would later author the *Zohar*. Unfortunately, many of these students did not treat each other with love and respect, and when a terrible plague swept through the land, all but a handful of them died. The *Zohar* tells us that there was a tremendous awakening of love after the tragedy. Rabbi Akiva himself came to his student Rav Shimon bar Yochai and said, "Make sure the basis of your teaching is love. Love is everything."

Rav Shimon took those words to heart, and years later, when he had students of his own, he saw to it that each time they met, they would give each other a hug. A tremendous amount of love was expressed because Rabbi Akiva begged Rav Shimon to make sure that he held fast to the teaching of *Ve'ahavta le'arecha kamocha ze klal gadol beTorah*, "Love your fellow man is the great precept of the Bible." Just as we saw with Nadav and Avihu, the sons of Aaron, love made it possible to go *acharei mot*, "after death."

Love also played a central role in the death of Rabbi Akiva. The *Talmud* says that although the Romans, who were in control of Israel at the time, had decreed that teaching the Torah was punishable by death, Rabbi Akiva continued to teach. The Romans arrested him and decided to execute him by peeling the skin off his body. As the torture began, Rabbi Akiva's students came to him and cried, "We cannot bear this! How can this be happening?" But Rabbi Akiva told his students that "according to the *Kriat Shema* (the Recitation of the *Shema* prayer), we must have love for the Creator, even if He takes our soul." Rabbi Akiva said, "I have been waiting for it my entire life, and now that I have the opportunity to live it, I want to do so." Then Rav Akiva spoke the words of the *Shema*, and as the last one left his lips, his soul left his body.

Rabbi Israel Friedman of Rhizin explains that when we say the *Shema* prayer in the morning and in the evening, our soul yearns for the level of *devekut* that is possible through this connection; of complete union with the Light of the Creator. So when Rabbi Akiva saw that the Romans were going to destroy his body, he recited the *Shema* and gave himself permission to let go of the last thing that separated his soul from the Creator. Rabbi Akiva's soul left his body because he chose not to hold it back any longer.

The *Zohar* says that as we connect to the deaths of Rabbi Akiva and the sons of Aaron, we are awakening the Light of the Creator within ourselves. This awareness of *devekut* as the purpose of our lives is the gift of this Shabbat of Acharei Mot-Kedoshim. Now for some of us, this concept may be frightening, but their deaths were not the deaths most people experience. As we've seen, they exercised the voluntary departure from the body available to the most righteous, the *tzadikim*, and our souls, too, can taste the same Light on the Shabbat of Acharei Mot-Kedoshim.

The *Talmud* tells us that when Moses ascended Mount Sinai to the Heavens to receive the gift of the Tablets, all the angels gave him gifts. The gift of the Angel of Death was the secret of the Light of the *ketoret* (incense). The *Zohar* explains that the word *ketoret* comes from the word *ketiru* or *hitkashrut*, which means "bonding." The secret power of the *ketoret* is revealed on this Shabbat because incense is the physical manifestation of the spiritual work of the *devekut* of Nadav and Avihu, who showed us that when we become completely unified with the Light of the Creator, we go "after death." When we recite the words of the *ketoret* connection from the *Siddur* (the prayer book), we connect to the Light that Nadav and Avihu revealed.

Rabbi Zadok HaKohen Rabinowitz, the *Pri Tzadik*, explains that although the Bible says that the Creator spoke to Moses after the death of the sons of Aaron, God didn't actually speak to Moses in words; instead, Moses suddenly felt something. The work that Nadav and Avihu had done filled Moses with the power of the *ketoret*. Indeed, if not for the unbelievable awakening of *devekut* through the actions of Nadav and Avihu, we would not have merited the Light of the *ketoret*. We could have lit incense all day and night, but the power of the Light of the incense would not have been revealed in our world.

The Shabbat of Acharei Mot-Kedoshim is one of the Shabbats that is not about arriving at a new understanding. It is a Shabbat that overwhelms us with *devekut*. It is the Shabbat when the level of being *acharei mot*, "after death," is revealed to us and to the world. It is the Shabbat of overwhelming Light, of overwhelming joy, of overwhelming love.

EMOR

Shabbat Emor precedes, and prepares us for, the Light revealed on *Lag B'Omer*, which marks the anniversary of the death of Rav Shimon bar Yochai, who wrote the *Zohar* while hiding from the Romans in a cave in the mountains. On *Lag B'Omer*, Rav Shimon gives us a taste of this Light, which is why *Lag B'Omer* is called the "Day of the Revelation of the Secrets." On *Lag B'Omer*, Rav Shimon is able to create an opening for us all to begin to have a sensual experience of the Light of the Creator. This is what *Lag B'Omer* is all about.

What does it mean when we say that Rav Shimon bar Yochai, through the *Zohar*, revealed its great secrets to our world? Most of us think that a secret is information that some people have and others do not. But the kabbalists explain that a secret is something that must *always* remain concealed. If I am able to share a secret, it is not truly a secret; it's just information that I have not yet shared. Yet on the day of his passing, Rav Shimon bar Yochai said, "I want to reveal all the secrets that I have not revealed my entire life." We know that the words spoken by Rav Shimon bar Yochai on the day he left this world are recorded in the chapter called *Idra Zuta*, the last revelations of Rav Shimon, in the *Zohar*. And we know that, according to the definition of Kabbalah, these are no longer secrets. So what was Rav Shimon bar Yochai referring to? What secrets can we connect to on *Lag B'Omer*?

The answer comes from the teachings of Rav Ashlag, who, you may recall, wrote that the purpose of our spiritual studies is to arrive at a level of consciousness where we can "taste and see that the Light of the Creator is good." At this level, we experience the Light—and the secrets that contain it—as sensation, as an intense feeling! When the kabbalists speak about secrets, they're not talking about words. If I am eating something sensational and I want to tell you how it tastes, I can certainly try, but even my most poetic and articulate words won't be able to fully convey my experience.

This taste, this experience of Light being revealed, is something we either feel or we don't. A secret, like a taste, is something that we cannot give over to someone else, no matter how hard we try. We can show them the way to get there, but we cannot give it to them directly. So when we talk about the secrets that Rav Shimon bar Yochai revealed in the *Zohar* on the day he left this world, we are not referring to the information he shared, but to the intense taste of Light that his students received. Shabbat Emor prepares us for the Light of *Lag B'Omer* by bringing our consciousness to the level of "tasting and seeing that the Light of the Creator is good." This is where we want to go.

We live on an enormous rock that rotates around the sun while hurtling through space at tremendous speed. But what causes the Earth to rotate on its own axis at the same time that it revolves around the sun? Scientists explain that there is no one natural force that causes the Earth to rotate around the sun, but rather two *opposing* forces. The first is the Earth's inertia—the tendency of an object to keep moving in a certain direction once it has started in that direction—and the force that opposes it is the gravitational pull of the sun. So there's a constant struggle between these two forces. If the gravitational pull of the sun had won the battle, the Earth would have crashed into the sun long ago; if it had lost, our planet would be drifting aimlessly through space.

So at the root of our physical existence lies a struggle between the nature of the Earth and the nature of the sun, a constant tension of desires that creates the perfect dynamic to support life. The *Arvei Nachal* says that this tension is also the foundation of our spiritual work. He explains that although many of us want our work to be easy, there are forces that oppose us. As we see, these obstacles actually serve an essential function, for only with constant opposition can we accomplish what we came to this world to do.

When we look at our lives—including our spiritual lives—we often separate our days into good and bad. On good days, we wake up in the morning excited and happy, and we continue that way. We make our connections, have great conversations, and help some people out; in short, we are being good spiritual people on those days. Then there are the days when we wake up cranky, and from that first moment things don't work at all well.

If we had to ask ourselves which days we're most proud of, we would point to those days when everything went well and we helped other people out. However, the *Arvei Nachal* tells us that those good days—those days when we think we reveal the most Light—are almost insignificant. As the *Zohar* says: "Light is only Light if it comes out of darkness." The *Arvei Nachal* explains that the Creator does not need us to be good people. There are millions of angels who are more spiritual than we will ever be, who wake up in the morning and are just Light all day. But we are not angels, and the Creator did not put us in this world to be all Light. We are in this world to bring Light out of darkness.

Most of us do not experience days that are either completely difficult or completely great; we usually spend a great deal of time bouncing back and forth. We might wake up in the morning and get a call from a friend who lives some distance away and needs help moving furniture. We might take time out of our busy day to make the long drive and then spend a few hours moving furniture. Because this is physical labor and precious time spent in aid of a friend, we feel that we are being spiritual and that this has therefore been a good day. But when we arrive home, our children immediately upset us and we quarrel with our spouse. While we are arguing, another friend calls us on the phone to ask a favor, but now we are short, almost rude, although helping this friend would take only take a few minutes. We know that what we have just done is reactive, but we make ourselves feel better by reminding ourselves of all those hours of sharing we did today.

The truth is that we have to completely change our understanding, because once again, those hours were not very significant. The few minutes when we were reactive with our family and our friend on the phone are the reason we are here in this world. If we can struggle through those moments and apologize, or call later to arrange an alternative and make amends, we will have turned things around. We will have revealed Light from darkness.

When we read the portion of Emor, it appears to contain many details that don't apply to our lives today. It begins by explaining whom the *Kohanim*, the priests, can marry and how the *Kohanim* can become impure or not pure. Then the portion introduces the various holidays we celebrate each year. On *Yom Kippur,* the tenth day of the month of *Tishrei,* the holiest day of the year, the Creator looks through our days, weeks, and months of the past year and makes a tally of our Light. Most of us would be shocked to see the Creator whiz through so many of our best hours and days, finding no Light. But if we questioned the Creator specifically about these six great hours here and those four hours there, the Creator would reply, "Those hours are not Light. Light is only Light that comes out of darkness."

The beauty of this understanding is that it allows us to completely change how we view our life. Those long hours of sharing, of connecting to the Light of the Creator, are not what matters. The only reason we are in this world is for those seconds and minutes of Light that we are able to pull out of darkness. This is what sustains us and our world. As the *Arvei Nachal* says, "Worthy are we if every day, we have a few minutes when we fight against the things that stop us, when we push ourselves to do the work we don't want to do."

BEHAR-BECHUKOTAI

Behar, the thirty-second reading from the Torah, is usually read in synagogue together with the following portion, Bechukotai. The word *behar*, which means "on the mountain," is used at the very beginning of the reading: "The Creator said to Moses on Mount Sinai...." This first portion describes the laws of the Sabbatical years, the Jubilee, and the Redemption. The word *bechukotai* means "in My Statutes" and appears in the first verse of the reading, which generally promises good things if the Torah is followed and negativity if spiritual principles are not followed.

In the portion of Behar, we read about *Shmittah*, a time when all the farmers' fields must remain fallow, or unworked, for an entire year. *Shmittah* occurs every seven years in the land of Israel. The Bible says that the Creator instructed Moses to speak to the Israelites at Mount Sinai and tell them: "Six years you shall sow your field, and six years you shall prune your vineyard and gather in the produce thereof. But the seventh year shall be a Sabbath of solemn rest for the land, a

Sabbath to God; you shall neither sow your field, nor prune your vineyard."

The obvious question considered in *Shmittah* is how people are going to feed themselves if they can't grow food on their land for an entire year. The Bible goes on to address this dilemma: "And if you shall say, 'What shall we eat in the seventh year?' … Then I will command My blessing upon you in the sixth year, and it shall bring forth produce for the three years. And you shall sow the eighth year, and eat of the produce, of the old store; until the ninth year, until her produce shall come in, you shall eat the old store."

According to Rabbi Elimelech of Lizhensk, the *Noam Elimelech*, in the portion of Behar, we gain not just an opening of blessings, but also the awakening of consciousness about the danger of doubt. This famous teaching from the *Noam Elimelech* and Rav Zusha reminds us that the Light of the Creator flows continuously for eternity, and if we never had any doubt about it, the Light would flow to us forever. But every time we do have doubt, we shut off the flow of the Light of the Creator.

Rabbi Shmuel Bornsztain, the *Shem Mishmuel*, adds that any Light that flows from the Upper Worlds to our world, even if the amount is small at first, becomes greater as it manifests. He explains that when we have complete certainty, untainted by any doubt, the Light that manifests is especially pure. The gift we receive on the Shabbat of Behar-Bechukotai is an opening to receive that kind of certainty—belief even when it seems illogical. Rav Ashlag calls this *emuna lamala min hada'at*, having certainty without understanding.

The *Shem Mishmuel* says that the fall that came after the sin of the Tree of Knowledge of Good and Evil in the Garden of Eden occurred for only one reason: lack of certainty. When tempted, Eve's internal serpent fell prey to the Satan's logic. She might have kept it simple. She could have told herself, "Even though there are many logical reasons why I *should* eat from the tree, I am going to rely instead on the words of the Creator." But because Eve began to wonder if the snake's position was right or wrong, she lost her way.

One of the great gifts of the Shabbat of Behar-Bechukotai is certainty—even when it doesn't make sense. Consider the *Shmittah* and the certainty required of people to sit and do no farming for a whole year, while the fields that feed their families are being overrun by weeds. *Shmittah* is about setting logic aside when we see something that makes no sense, knowing that this situation comes to us from the Creator and, therefore, is in our best interest. When we do this, then we are *tamim, im HaShem haElokecha* (simple, and with the Creator).

What is the gift of the consciousness of *Shmittah*? *Shmittah* allows us to see something that makes absolutely no sense to us and say, "I know that this is coming from the Creator; therefore, it is the best thing for me." However, the *Galut*, the Exile, continues because, instead of *Shmittah*, we want our work to make logical sense. In one of his many letters to my father, Rav Brandwein quotes the verse: "The Creator will not hold back any blessings from the one who walks simply...." Once we have complete certainty—which is not easy to develop—we realize that even the small things that don't make sense, that go against everything that seems right, come to us from the Creator—and therefore make us happy. As Rav Brandwein constantly told my father, the Rav, once we achieve complete certainty and act on it time and time again, eventually the Creator cannot stop an abundance of Light and blessings from coming to us. Then we will not only be keepers of *Shmittah*, not only will we accept things that don't make sense, but we will be full of joy because of them.

Before the wisdom of the Baal Shem Tov had been revealed to the world, he would travel from city to city and from village to village, teaching a little bit here and a little bit there. Sometimes he would teach children the Hebrew alphabet; sometimes he would teach adults. On one such trip, he came to a village where he received a message that he needed to go speak to the man of a specific house. He arrived at the house and knocked on the door. The wife of the man welcomed him in and asked him to have a seat until her husband returned from the synagogue.

The Baal Shem Tov sat there and waited for hours. Finally, a simple man walked into the house. The Baal Shem Tov asked him, "What took you so long? What have you been doing all this time?" The simple man answered, "I'm a little embarrassed to admit it, but I don't know how to pray. In the prayer book, there are morning prayers, afternoon prayers, evening prayers, and Shabbat prayers. There are so many prayers to be said at different times that I have no idea where these prayers begin or end. So what do I do? Every morning, I take the prayer book and just read it all the way through."

The Baal Shem Tov replied, "Oh, so this is probably why I am here. I received a message that I'm supposed to come and teach you. Let me sit down and show you where the prayers begin and end so you won't have to spend so many hours every day reading the entire prayer book." And they sat down with paper and pencil, and together, the Baal Shem Tov and the simple man made notes. Once they were done, the simple man stuck all the sheets of instructions into the appropriate places in the prayer book.

Content that he had accomplished what he had set out to do, the Baal Shem Tov left the simple man's home. Half an hour later, the man's children were playing in the house and knocked the prayer book off the table onto the floor. All the papers indicating the order of the prayers fell out. Upset, the man turned to his children and said, "This wise scholar came and spent a lot of time showing me how to do the prayers the right way, so now what am I going to do?" The simple man decided to run after the Baal Shem Tov. At first, he didn't know which way to go, but people along the way directed him.

Meanwhile, the Baal Shem Tov had arrived at a very large river with a strong current that made it difficult to cross. He dismounted, took his handkerchief from his jacket pocket, and placed it on the river. With that, he was able to walk on top of the water across the river to the opposite shore. The simple man arrived at the river just in time to see what the Baal Shem Tov had done, so he, too, took out his handkerchief, placed it on the river, and walked across. Then he ran after the Baal Shem Tov, shouting, "Teacher, teacher, please stop!" The Baal Shem Tov turned around. The simple man ran up to him and said, "After you left, my children accidently knocked my prayer book onto the floor. All the papers fell out, and now I don't know what to do."

The Baal Shem Tov looked back and said, "I don't understand. How did you find me? How did you cross the river?" The man answered, "Well, I saw that before you crossed it, you took out your handkerchief and placed it on the water, so I just did the same thing." The Baal Shem Tov regarded the man thoughtfully for a few moments and said, "You know what? I think your prayers are exactly right just as they are."

The negative side wants us to think, *I don't do this or that just right, so I can't be an amazing channel for blessing for others.* However, the Baal Shem Tov teaches us that there is unbelievable power in simplicity, certainty, and purity of heart. The *Midrash* says that the Redemption will come through the keepers of *Shmittah.* Certainty that defies logic is one of the keys to bringing about the Redemption.

When I was in Israel recently, I went to the grave of the *Arvei Nachal* in Safed. He was a student of the Baal Shem Tov, and the beauty of his teachings is that he delves deeper into things that we already think we know, and what he shows us there can really change our lives.

In our study of *Ten Luminous Emanations* by Rav Ashlag, we learn that within each of the Five Worlds, there are Ten *Sefirot,* or ten realms, each of which contains within itself another Ten *Sefirot,* and within each of these *Sefirot* lie yet another Ten *Sefirot,* and so on, endlessly. The *Arvei Nachal* asks, "Why do we have an endless number of worlds?" To answer this question, he quotes the Ramchal, who says that the ultimate state of knowledge is to come to the understanding that we really don't know anything, that no matter what we have learned so far, it is nothing compared to true understanding.

The *Arvei Nachal* goes on to say that the only way our spiritual work actually reveals Light is if we diminish ourselves in everything that we do—that the purpose of all our spiritual work is this consciousness of lowering ourselves. As an example, he looks at the way nature works, at the way trees and other vegetation grow from seeds. The Light of growth exists in all the earth, but there has to be a *tzimtzum*, a diminishment of the Light in a specific point, a deterioration of the shell around the seed before it can draw all the Light of growth from the earth and become a plant or tree.

The same is true of us. Our shell has to break, too, before any of the Light of growth that exists in the earth around us can be revealed.

Rav Ashlag uses the parable of a little worm inside an apple to develop this idea. This worm thinks his life is nothing but dark and cold, but still he continues to eat his way through the apple. Then, at some point, he bites through the skin of the apple and suddenly, light floods in all around. The little worm crawls out and gazes at the great big world, stunned to find that life is not so dark and cold after all.

The same is true of our spiritual growth. If we are doing our work properly, it feels as if we are climbing through an old system of mines inside a mountain, breaking through many tunnels and elevating to different levels, yet always aware of the many feet we still have to go, no matter how many we have already climbed. When the Ramchal speaks about "knowing that we don't know," he isn't referring to our studies, but to the diminishment of ego, to the feeling that the spiritual rules may not make sense to us but we work within them anyway, always aware that whatever spiritual distance we may have traveled, there are countless worlds yet to go.

At its core, the purpose of the spiritual work that we do is to understand that we may have accomplished something, but compared to what the Creator is showing us we still need to accomplish, we have done nothing. The Ramchal says that through this consciousness, we achieve *devekut* (unification) with the Light of the Creator, that doing this work is how we grow. The *Zohar* says that if we see our spiritual work as nothing, we have done a lot. Why? Because this is a sign of how much we've grown.

The point I wish to make is that sometimes we think of diminishing our ego as a nice addition to our spiritual work, or even an important addition to our spiritual work. But what the *Arvei Nachal* is telling us here is that if diminishing our ego is not at the heart of our spiritual life, we are accomplishing nothing.

We have to be careful, however, to avoid the trap of thinking we have done nothing and feeling depressed about it. This state of mind is not about guilt or shame for not doing more. It's just about accepting that what we have done is nothing compared to what remains to be done—a level of surrender that comes from tremendous spiritual work, and brings with it tremendous joy and inspiration. It is a gift from the Creator to be aware of how much further there is to go. Surrendering to this awareness is what breaks open our shell and allows the Light that we reveal to enter. By minimizing our self-importance we make room for the Creator to join us, so that this sense that our journey is endless is accompanied by sheer delight in that journey. And when we feel this way, it's a sure sign that we are growing.

At the beginning of this chapter, we began our discussion with the *Arvei Nachal*'s question: "Why are there so many worlds?" Now we understand the beauty in his answer: "The reason there are so many worlds is because this way, there is literally an endless amount of travel, an endless amount of growth."

NUMBERS

BAMIDBAR

Bamidbar, which means "in the wilderness," is the first portion in Book of Numbers. It comes from the beginning of the first verse: "Then the Creator spoke to Moses in the wilderness of Sinai…." The Book of Numbers tells the story of the Israelites' journey through the wilderness on their way to the Promised Land, their spiritual fall just as they were about to enter the land, and their subsequent forty years of wandering. The Book of Numbers ends with the Israelites back at the borders of Canaan, ready once again to take what the Creator has told them is their inheritance.

The Bible tells us that the Creator came to Moses in the Sinai desert and said, "Take you the sum of all the congregation of the Children of Israel, after their families, by the house of their fathers, with the number of their names, every male by their polls." According to the kabbalists, the Creator was not asking Moses to count people the way we usually do. Our system is inaccurate: We see an individual as one person; we see a couple and count them as two people; and so on. But the spiritual number associated with one person may be very different. Rav Ashlag explains that one righteous person may be surrounded by tens of thousands of souls. While most of us cannot see the souls attached to a person, Moses could, and so could Aaron.

One way of assessing a person's spiritual worth is by the number of souls that surround them. Rabbi Shlomo HaKohen of Radomsk, the *Tiferet Shlomo*, tells us that we also create an angel with every spiritual action that we perform. The Creator told Moses and Aaron, "From twenty years old and upward, all that are able to go forth to war in Israel, you and Aaron shall number them by their armies." The *Tiferet Shlomo* says that the expression "those who go forth to war" refers to these angels.

According to the *Tiferet Shlomo*, we create angels during the week through our actions and our words, but these angels have only a body without a soul. However, when we make our connection to the song *Shalom Aleichem* ("Peace unto you, ministering angels") on Friday night each Shabbat, these angels receive their souls. If a person creates a hundred angels during the week but does not make his or her connection to *Shalom Aleichem*, he or she has created dead angels—bodies uninhabited by souls. When we feel excitement about the approaching Shabbat, part of this excitement is due to our angels who know they are about to receive their souls—they are about to become alive! I think about this every Friday night when we sing *Shalom Aleichem*.

The portion of Bamidbar is always read on the Shabbat prior to *Shavuot*, indicating that what we learn about connecting to the Light of the Shabbat of Bamidbar will be helpful, not just for this Shabbat but also for *Shavuot*.

To explain the inner meaning of the biblical verse: "And with you, there shall be a man of every tribe; every one head of the house of his fathers," the *Tiferet Shlomo* cites from a *Mishnah* in *Pirkei Avot* (*Ethics of Our Fathers*), which says: "Let your home be a meeting place for the wise, dust yourself in the soil of their feet, and drink thirstily of their words." At first, this doesn't seem to make much sense. The *Tiferet Shlomo* asks, "Are not the scholars being told that their homes should be gathering places for scholars? If so, the obvious question among the scholars would be: 'Why would I go to your house when I'm supposed to be bringing everyone to my home?'"

So what does this *Mishnah* mean? The *Tiferet Shlomo* explains it this way: If a person performs a spiritual action in the proper way, that person can connect to the soul of a righteous person, a *tzadik*, who has left this world. Another way we access souls beyond our own is when we receive an *ibur*, a spark of a righteous soul. Rav Ashlag, in his *Sulam* commentary on the *Zohar*, makes it clear that we cannot grow spiritually without this spark from a righteous soul. Working on our own is not enough.

There are three ways we can merit an *ibur*. The first is by performing the same action that a specific righteous person was known for. For instance, part of Rabbi Pinchas ben Yair's greatness was his ability to share unconditionally. So if a person undertakes an act of unconditional sharing, he or she can receive an *ibur* from the soul of Rabbi Pinchas ben Yair. Or if a person acts with great humility, which was one of the qualities of Moses, he or she can receive a spark of the Light of Moses.

The second way to receive an *ibur* is through study. When we study the words of a righteous person, we can also receive a spark of his or her soul. The Baal Shem Tov repeatedly warned, however, that we have to bring both clarity and certainty to this process because our consciousness influences the degree to which it occurs. On the Shabbat of Bamidbar when we read that Moses and Aaron come to awaken us, our clarity about this helps make it happen. Similarly, when we read from the *Zohar*, it is our certainty that in the process we are receiving a spark of the soul of Rav Shimon bar Yochai that influences our ability to accept that *ibur*.

As we've seen, the third way to receive an *ibur* is to visit the graves of righteous souls. Rabbi Chaim Vital wrote that his teacher, the Ari, would often send him to a specific righteous person's grave with a particular meditation for a certain kind of help. One of the reasons I always get excited about going to Israel is the joy of receiving *iburim* at the graves of the righteous.

So when the *Pirkei Avot* says: "Let your home be a meeting place for the wise," one way to interpret this is metaphysical: We should strive to be receptive, to be "a meeting place" for sparks from the souls of the righteous. We read the portion of Bamidbar before *Shavuot* because it prepares us to receive the Light of the Tree of Life on *Shavuot*. Why? Because Bamidbar is the Shabbat of *iburim*, the Shabbat when the Creator tells Moses and Aaron to come down and infuse sparks of their souls into everyone who truly awakens a desire for growth and change. This is the Shabbat when we sow the seeds for *iburim* for this entire year: If we merit connecting to the power of an *ibur* on the Shabbat of Bamidbar, we move closer to the Light of *Shavuot*, the removal of death from our world.

On the surface, this portion is about counting a group of Israelites a few thousand years ago, but on a deeper level, the Creator is telling Moses and Aaron that they should gather all the righteous souls from time immemorial and prepare them to come down to those of us ready to receive an *ibur*, not just on this Shabbat of Bamidbar, but at any time this year. Because Moses and Aaron were able to see a person's true spiritual worth, they were the ones chosen for this role.

The *Zohar* says that when the Israelites went out of Egypt, the positive forces in the world became stronger and the moon shone, causing the forces of darkness to be diminished in the world. This gave the Creator the opportunity to send the Israelites into the desert without harm. My father, the Rav, describes the desert as the place where the *sitra achra*, the negative side, has dominion. When the Creator saw an opening to finish off the darkness at the very place where its forces were greatest, He prepared the Israelites for a great battle. The Shabbat of Bamidbar braces us for the *naso et rosh*—the "raising of the head" or "lifting up" as the Torah calls it in the next portion—and gives each of us strength.

As we come closer to *Shavuot*, the Creator gives each of us, to whatever degree we are ready to receive it, the strength to finish off the negative side. Rabbi Shmuel Bornsztain, the *Shem Mishmuel* says we have to imagine that the whole world depends on our spiritual work. Fortunately, on the Shabbat of Bamidbar, Moses and Aaron come to each of us and awaken a sense of how vitally important we and our spiritual work really are.

There is an interesting section in the *Midrash* that has to do with both the portion of Bamidbar and *Shavuot*. The *Talmud* says that when the Israelites left the town of Refidim and arrived at Mount Sinai, the place in the desert where they were to receive the Torah, they suffered from what is referred to as "weakness from the travel." What does this mean? Rabbi Yitzchak Myer Alter, the *Chidushei HaRim*, explains that the "weakness from the travel" is the power of *amalek*, the source of the voice inside our head that says we don't deserve something.

The *Midrash* explains that when the Israelites arrived at Mount Sinai, they gave up. But why now? They had been through the miracle of the plagues. They had been freed from Egypt. They had escaped Pharaoh's chariots, thanks to the miraculous parting of the Red Sea. Now that they were at the mountain—now that they were just about to receive the Light of the Tree of Life—why would they give up? This doesn't make sense. It's as if a ship traveling across a vast ocean comes within sight of its port city and suddenly decides to turn around. Why give up now? Why not when the ship was in the middle of the ocean, having traveled for weeks with no sight of land?

The *Shem Mishmuel* gives a great explanation for this seemingly inexplicable behavior of the Israelites at Mount Sinai: "These people had common sense. They understood that if they were going to connect to the Light of the Tree of Life, they would have to be very pure, very holy, and very connected. And they saw that they had to do this by the next day. But when they looked inside themselves, they realized that they were not ready. They didn't give up because they were daunted by physical hardship or danger; they gave up because they had clarity about the fact that they were nowhere near spiritually ready to receive this great revelation."

We fall prey to logic like this all the time. Instead of thinking, *If this is what is supposed to happen, I'll go with it*, we let rationality get in the way. If the Creator came to tell us that we were going to receive immortality tomorrow, would we say, "Wait a second, let me think about this. Am I ready?" Instead of being so rational, I'd hope we'd be excited and be able to tell ourselves, "You know, this does not make a bit of sense, but how often do I get a chance like this?"

At Mount Sinai after the sin of the golden calf, the Israelites said, "We don't deserve the Light of *bila hamavet lanetzach*; we are not ready." What they should have said was, "Forget logic. Forget what we do and don't deserve. The Creator says we are going to receive this gift, so we need to accept it." Like the Israelites we, too, diminish our chances for redemption, for miracles, for blessings, because we think we are not ready. Don't let yourself fall victim to the debilitating logic of *amalek*, the negative side. Throw out that call for doubt and delay. Ignore that voice that we hear all too often that says, "Have I and my generation really done enough to bring an end to pain, suffering, and death in the world?"

Kabbalists have always said that if enough people had certainty, the Final Redemption would come. But what happens? Logic intervenes, and we think, *I don't deserve it; I'm not ready.* So let's be less logical. The Light we have revealed is enough. The Redemption can come with *Shavuot* this year. Such is the power of certainty.

Almost every night, my children ask me to read them a story before they go to bed. A few nights ago, my daughter Miriam asked me to tell her a story about the Baal Shem Tov. I told her one that I have heard many times before, but the way I "tasted it" this time was different from any other.

It came to the attention of the Baal Shem Tov that there was someone known as "the shepherd" whose spiritual work was greater than the Baal Shem Tov's own, so he decided to go and meet this person. The Baal Shem Tov and his students got into his carriage and travelled to the village where this man lived. When they arrived, they saw the shepherd tending his flock nearby, so they stood where he wouldn't notice them observing him. As the shepherd stood in the field where his sheep were grazing, he turned his face up to the

Heavens, and said to the Creator, "I love You so much, but as You know, I'm a very simple person. I don't even know how to read. But I do have this shepherd's whistle and I know how to blow it, so I'm asking that this be acceptable before You."

With that, the shepherd blew the whistle with all his might for a long time, until finally he fainted. When he came around, he got up again and said to the Creator, "I love You so much that I want to do something more for You, so this time I'm going to dance." He then cavorted with all his energy, until, after an hour, he fell to the ground in total exhaustion. After he recovered, he got up and said to the Creator, "I love You so much that I want to do yet more for You, but as you know, I am a poor, simple man. Still, I have a penny in my pocket." He took the penny and threw it up toward Heaven with all his might. At that moment, to their complete astonishment, the Baal Shem Tov and his students saw a hand come out from the Heavens and catch the penny.

The Baal Shem Tov turned to his students and said, "Until this day, I thought I knew what spiritual work was. But now, for the first time in my life, I see how wrong I was. When we love the Creator in this moment with everything we have, we forget all about not being deserving. If, like the shepherd, I could put all my love into one action on behalf of the Creator, I would see that it is more than enough!"

That night, after reading this story to my children, I was about to do the Counting of the Omer, but I felt too tired. Then the story of the Baal Shem Tov came to mind, and I knew that the Counting of the Omer could put me in direct contact with the Creator if I could just put everything into it.

NASO

The biblical portion of Naso, meaning "lift up," takes its name from the first words of the second verse of the Hebrew, which say: "Lift up the heads of the sons of Gershon," referring to the Creator's desire to have the sons of Gershon counted. The importance of the Shabbat of Naso is connected to the fact that it follows *Shavuot*, which itself has such phenomenal energy that it is divided into two parts.

On the night before *Shavuot*, we are given new senses: A new heart, a new spirit, a new ability to truly taste and feel the Light of the Creator. If we merit this gift on the night of *Shavuot*—and hopefully, we do—we transform how we connect to the Light of the Creator. Rav Ashlag explains that this is an opening when the Creator gives us amazing gifts from the Supernal Worlds, but it takes time for us to receive these gifts once they have been given. This is why *Shavuot* has two parts: The night before *Shavuot*, we are given the faculties with which to taste what is coming, and the next morning of *Shavuot*, we are given the Light itself.

We need the first gift in order to appreciate the second, much the way a toddler would only appreciate a piece of cake in a glass case if the next gift was the key. It takes a little while for the reality of our new circumstances to sink in. We are given instructions and an amazingly powerful new spiritual vehicle on *Shavuot*, but we don't realize what we have until the portion of Naso.

The *Zohar* gives special prominence to the portion of Naso, linking it to the revelation of the *Idra Rabba*, the Great Assembly. The word *idra* in Aramaic means "room or assembly." The Great Assembly occurred when Rav Shimon bar Yochai, the author of the *Zohar*, gathered nine other scholars in the sacred *Idra* Cave, west of the city of Safed in Israel, to thresh out all the secrets of the Torah. This was the first time in history when all the secrets of the universe were revealed. The other secrets in the *Zohar* are only pieces of the great revelation of the *Idra Rabba*.

The Torah reading on *Shavuot* discusses the giving of the Ten Utterances (the Torah) on Mount Sinai. We also read the Haftarah, a section from the Book of Prophets, following the Torah portion. The Haftarah for *Shavuot* speaks of Ezekiel's vision of the angels, when he is actually sensing the Light of the Creator. At one time, I had difficulty understanding this Haftarah's correlation to the Torah reading for *Shavuot*, but now I see that when we connect to the Torah reading and to the Haftarah on *Shavuot*, we are meant to achieve a certain level of prophecy. First, we receive the gift of being able to taste the Light of the Creator, and then we are given the connection to the Torah itself—to *Etz HaChaim*, the Tree of Life. The next step after this is to establish this connection as a constant in our lives through our new power of prophecy—the power of being able to give and to receive messages from the Light of the Creator.

Now that we realize what is being given to us on *Shavuot*, we can see why the *Idra Rabba*, the great revelation of Rav Shimon bar Yochai, was given on the Shabbat of Naso. Because the Shabbat of Naso follows *Shavuot*, it provides us with time to absorb and to connect to these secrets. When Rav Shimon bar Yochai says it's time to reveal all the secrets of the Torah, he doesn't mean that it's time to reveal information that we didn't previously have, but rather, thanks to the gifts of *Shavuot*, it's an opportunity to finally *taste* all of these secrets. All the necessary elements fall into place on the Shabbat of Naso.

Some time ago, I took my family to Jerusalem and I went to my favorite place, the grave of Rav Ashlag. While I was there, I made what I felt was a very strong connection, so I asked Rav Ashlag for a message. But when I closed my eyes, all I could see was a man's beard. I opened and closed my eyes several times, but still the image didn't change. I thought perhaps Rav Ashlag was trying to tell me something about himself, so I closed my eyes for a long time, trying to see the rest of what seemed to be Rav Ashlag's face. Nothing doing. No matter how hard I tried, I kept seeing a man's beard, no more and no less. I knew something significant was happening, but for some reason, I wasn't getting the message.

The Ari says that once we have finished reading from the Torah and the Prophets on *Shavuot*, we should read as much as we can from the secrets of the *Zohar*. A few days after my visit to Rav Ashlag's grave, on the holiday of *Shavuot*, I began reading from the *Zohar*, when suddenly I understood! Thanks to the gift of *Shavuot*, I realized that what Rav Ashlag was showing me, as I stood at his gravesite, was that I needed to study a specific section of the *Idra Rabba*, a passage called the "Thirteen Corrections of the Supernal Beard." Those pages turned out to have a very special meaning for me, and the whole experience provided me with an awesome taste of the Light of the Creator.

The reason I'm sharing this with you is because I think that on the week leading up to the Shabbat of Naso, we can all raise our level of desire. Amazing things are possible at this time. It is a time of revelations, both around us and within us. When we actually taste the Light of the Creator instead of just learning about it, we can never go back to being the person we were before. A shift in consciousness has taken place that cannot be reversed. As the kabbalists say, "The person that I need to become is not simply a better version of me; it is a new, concealed, secret, completely different self."

The gift of *Shavuot* that continues into the Shabbat of Naso is the opportunity for us to become a completely different self, a self that lies far beyond anything that we can even imagine today. And the gates to that gift are opened to us on the Shabbat of Naso.

I would like to share a story about the Baal Shem Tov that relates to the revelation we have been discussing, but before I begin, it's important to note that there were different stages in this great kabbalist's life. During the first part of the Baal Shem Tov's life, he was a *tzadik nistar* (a concealed righteous person): He traveled the world, but let few people see his true greatness.

When the Baal Shem Tov began teaching and disseminating wisdom, he received a message by *Ruach HaKodesh*, or Divine Inspiration, that Rav Dov Ber, the Magid of Mezritch, needed to become his student. The Baal Shem Tov did not know what to do with this message because Rav Dov Ber was a very wise man, who had been studying his entire life, and he was known to have what we might call a healthy ego. There was no logical way Rav Dov Ber would want to come and study from the Baal Shem Tov.

However, Rav Dov Ber had a persistent problem with his leg, and the doctors were at a loss to help him. His wife suggested that he go and see this wise man called the Baal Shem Tov, whom she had recently heard about. But Rav Dov Ber was reluctant to take her suggestion, since he himself did not know the Baal Shem Tov. As Rav Dov Ber told his wife, "Some people may be excited about the Baal Shem Tov, but I have been studying and praying my entire life, so I doubt this newcomer is going to be able to help me."

Meanwhile, however, his leg steadily grew worse, to the point where the pain was interfering with his spiritual work and he was no longer even able to go to the *mikveh*, the ritual bath. His wife kept insisting that he visit the Baal Shem Tov, and eventually, Rav Dov Ber agreed to ask for his help. A few days later, he set off in his carriage for the town of Mezibuz, where the Baal Shem Tov lived. When he arrived at the Baal Shem Tov's home, the Baal Shem Tov's attendant told his master that there was a great wise man to see him, and Rav Dov Ber was shown into the Baal Shem Tov's sitting room.

Without preamble, the Baal Shem Tov launched into a long story about traveling a few weeks before and how worried he had been that it would be difficult to find food for Alexi, his carriage driver. Finally, the Baal Shem Tov concluded by saying, "But, thank God, toward the end of the day, we stopped at a village and we found food for Alexi to eat." With that, the Baal Shem Tov rose, showed his guest to the door, and bade him good afternoon.

As Rav Dov Ber walked out, he was very upset. He thought, *The Baal Shem Tov cannot help me; he is an idiot.* Rav Dov Ber had traveled all this distance, expecting to hear some words of wisdom, some secrets that might help him, and all the Baal Shem Tov had told him was a story about not being sure he could find food for his carriage driver. What sort of nonsense was this?

Rav Dov Ber left the Baal Shem Tov's home and went straight to his carriage driver, instructing him to prepare to leave. His carriage driver advised his master against leaving right away, counseling that it would be safer to find lodgings in Mezibuz and to leave first thing in the morning. The highway was no place to be in the middle of the night.

Still upset by what had transpired, Rav Dov Ber reluctantly agreed to spend the night in Mezibuz and leave first thing in the morning. At six o'clock that evening, however, the attendant of the Baal Shem Tov came to the door of the inn where Rav Dov Ber was staying and said, "My master and teacher, the Baal Shem Tov, would like to see you." Knowing that he was stuck in Mezibuz overnight anyway, Rav Dov Ber decided he had nothing to lose by going back to visit the Baal Shem Tov.

Once Rav Dov Ber was at the Baal Shem Tov's home, the Baal Shem Tov said, "You know, I forgot to tell you, but on the same trip that I was talking to you about earlier, we also forgot to pack hay for the horses. So needless to say, I was concerned that we weren't going to have food for the horses to eat either. But, thank God, in that same village where we found food for Alexi, there was also hay for our animals. I just wanted to make sure I didn't forget to tell you that."

Rav Dov Ber walked out a second time, more confused and annoyed than before. He wondered how anyone could possibly see anything in this Baal Shem Tov. The man was obviously dim-witted. He went back to the inn and studied and prayed, trying to gain some Light from what was turning out to be a wasted trip.

Around midnight, there was a knock on his door, and again it was the Baal Shem Tov's attendant. "My teacher and master, the Baal Shem Tov, wants you to come and visit him." Rav Dov Ber thought, *Did the Baal Shem Tov still not tell me all the details of that trip? Still, since I'm stuck here for the night, I might as well go.*

When he arrived at the Baal Shem Tov's home, the Baal Shem Tov asked him, "Do you ever study the *Writings of the Ari*, by Rav Isaac Luria, the great kabbalist?" The Magid of Mezritch answered, "Of course. I have been studying these writings my entire life." The Baal Shem Tov then handed him the volume called *Pri Etz HaChaim* (*The Tree of Life*) and asked the Magid to read a certain passage and explain it to him. Rav Dov Ber noticed that the particular section the Baal Shem Tov had chosen was one that he had, in fact, studied extensively. The Magid read the passage aloud very slowly so that the Baal Shem Tov could follow what he was reading, and then launched into a long explanation of what he had just read.

In the middle of the Magid's explanation, the Baal Shem Tov grabbed the book away from him, saying, "Everything you have said is completely wrong." The Baal Shem Tov then began reading the same pages, but as he uttered the words, Light came into the room. And when the Baal Shem Tov spoke the names of the angels mentioned by the Ari, those very angels entered the room as well. The Magid was so overwhelmed that he fainted.

The Baal Shem Tov closed the *Pri Etz HaChaim* from the *Writings of the Ari* and set it back on the shelf. When Rav Dov Ber came to, the Baal Shem Tov told him, "You have to understand that although you have studied your entire life, all you have is knowledge. Your learning has no soul. It means nothing if you're not able to inject

Light into it." From that moment on, the Magid of Mezritch became the Baal Shem Tov's most devoted student.

The gift of tasting the Light of the Creator is given to us on *Shavuot*, and to manifest it—to truly make it a part of our life—we cannot be content with what went before. We do not want the Shabbat of Naso to simply give us something in addition to what we are already. We want to become a new person, one who senses, feels, tastes, and sees the Light in everything. This is the opportunity we are given on the Shabbat of Naso.

BEHA'ALOTCHA

Throughout the history of Kabbalah—a wisdom that has been shrouded in secrecy for centuries—a handful of people, including Rav Shimon bar Yochai, Rav Isaac Luria (the Ari), and Rav Ashlag, have devoted themselves to bringing about the *Gemar HaTikkun*, the Final Correction, by sharing this wisdom with the world. Still, the reason great kabbalists do their spiritual work is not to achieve things in this world. Their work may take place here, but the reason they do it is to reveal Light in the Upper Worlds.

A case in point is that of the great kabbalist, the Komarno Rebbe, Rabbi Yitzchak Isaac of Komarno, who wrote a remarkable, very detailed commentary on the Torah called *Heichal HaBrachah* (*The Chamber of Blessings*), which is rarely studied today. However, if you could ask Rabbi Yitzchak Isaac right now how he feels about so few people reading the *Heichal HaBrachah* after he spent years on these teachings, I would guess he'd say that it doesn't bother him at all. Why? Because his reason for coming up with this wisdom was not to attract a wide readership, but because the very act of understanding and writing revealed so much Light in the Upper Worlds.

To help us better understand this point, we turn to the portion of Beha'alotcha ("when you ascend,") which begins with the line: "And God spoke to Moses, saying, 'Speak to Aaron, and say to him, When you light the lamps, the seven lamps shall give light in front of the *Menorah*.'" The *Midrash* explains that Aaron was worried because the leaders of the other tribes had brought twelve sacrifices to the Tabernacle and he had brought nothing. But the Creator told Aaron not to worry, for when he lit the *Menorah* in the Tabernacle, its Light was going to last forever. But the biblical commentators ask how the Creator could say that? Surely once the Tabernacle no longer existed, the candles would be lit no longer.

Rabbi Moshe Alshich, the Alshich HaKadosh, a great kabbalist living in Safed at the time of Rabbi Isaac Luria, tells us that by lighting the *Menorah* in the Tabernacle at the Creator's request, Aaron also lit up the Upper Worlds. And that Light is what will continue to shine until the coming of the Messiah. Any act that reveals Light has a physical manifestation, but there is a much deeper level of satisfaction available to us in the knowledge that we are revealing Light in the Upper Worlds. Focusing on the Upper Worlds leads to an amazing shift of consciousness—suddenly, how many people we help or whether or not people like what we are doing (or even know about what we are doing) doesn't even enter the equation.

This is how Rabbi Yitzchak Isaac of Komarna could write an entire commentary on the Torah and not care if it had any future readers; like Aaron, he was lighting the *Menorah* in the Upper Worlds that shines forever.

A brief story about the Baal Shem Tov further illustrates this point.

The Baal Shem Tov once came to a synagogue, but rather than enter, he just stood by the door. When a congregant approached and asked him why he did not go inside, the Baal Shem Tov replied, "Because the room is filled with people's prayers." When the man said, "Isn't that as it should be?" the Baal Shem Tov said, "Our prayers are meant to travel up into the Upper Worlds. When we pray with love and awe, our prayers rise. But when we pray without this consciousness, it literally weighs down our prayers, keeping them in this world. I find it difficult to pray in a room full of unelevated prayers."

In the *Heichal HaBrachah*, Rabbi Yitzchak Isaac of Komarno discusses the famous story in the portion of Beha'alotcha where Aaron and Miriam spoke negatively about Moses, resulting in Miriam's leprosy. The Bible says: "Moses cried out to the Creator, saying, '*El na refa na lah.*'" In his commentary, Rabbi Yitzchak Isaac spends a lot of time discussing why certain words and letters appear as they do in the Torah, and in this case, he expresses his desire to understand why the word *na* or "please," appears twice in the phrase Moses used to heal his sister: The word *El* is a Name of God, *na* means "please," *refa* means "heal," *na* means "please," and *la* means "her," referring to his sister, Miriam, who had leprosy.

Rabbi Yitzchak Isaac begins his investigation by saying, "I learned from my teacher that all our prayers should only be for the *Shechinah*, with the consciousness of 'not for our world.' Why does a person get sick in this world? Because there is a lack in the *Shechinah*. Why does a person need food or money in this world? Only because there is a lack in the *Shechinah*. Every lack that we see in a person's life is only there because of a lack in the Upper World."

But how can we talk about a lack in the *Shechinah* when we know that the Light has no lack? Rav Ashlag explains that within the Light of the Creator, there is no lack, but the *Shechinah* is an intermediary level of Light created specifically for the purpose of being with the Israelites during their exile—and with us in ours. Part of the *Shechinah*'s purpose is to lack when we lack.

Rabbi Yitzchak Isaac says, "But truly, the intention of our prayer should never be for us or another person. It should be: 'Please, Creator, allow my prayers to fill that specific lack in the *Shechinah*. I know that if that specific lack is filled in the *Shechinah*, the manifestation of that specific lack in our physical world will be filled.'" This may sound like a minor shift in attitude, but it means that we now have a way to make our prayers far more powerful. Rabbi Yitzchak Isaac puts it this way: "How was the Baal Shem Tov able to create miracles that were not known or revealed in the world from the time of the *Tannaim* [70–200 CE] until the time of the Baal Shem Tov [17th century]? It was not his greatness that cured the deathly ill. It was not his purity that helped the blind man see. It was not his wisdom or connection to the Light of the Creator that brought the blessing of children to those who could not conceive. These wondrous things happened because the Baal Shem Tov never prayed for a single person. He prayed only that the *Shechinah* should be filled with Light, and in this way, he was able to perform miracles that had never existed before."

Like the Baal Shem Tov, we can create miracles if we make this shift in emphasis from this world to focus on the Upper Worlds. Rabbi Yitzchak Isaac says, "I know we cannot do this all the time. Sometimes a person can get so involved in their own sadness that they cannot even think about the pain of the *Shechinah*. But we must know that, even in these times, we will be answered more quickly if we are able to put our focus to the Supernal lack in the *Shechinah*. Even when we are in great pain, we can say, 'Master of the World, my pain is great, but I also feel the Supernal pain and therefore, I am asking for both to be healed.'"

This elevated prayer of healing is mentioned for the first time in the Torah when Moses stands in front of his sick sister, Miriam, knowing that her leprosy is a manifestation of something lacking in the Supernal order, in the *Shechinah*. Therefore, his first prayer is for the *Shechinah*, which is an aspect of the Creator: *El na refa*, "God, please heal." But because Moses also feels great pain for his sister, his prayer is also for her: *na la*, "please, her." *El na refa na la* teaches us that our first desire needs to be to heal the lack in the *Shechinah*, and only then to let the healing flow down to the person who needs it. Here, in the portion of Beha'alotcha, Moses teaches us—and all future generations—how to pray.

What is the hallmark of people who place their emphasis on the Upper Worlds? Humility. In the portion of Beha'alotcha, the Bible says: "Now the man Moses was very humble, the most humble man on the face of the Earth." I used to think when I read this portion, *We have all heard so much about the importance of diminishing the ego, of being humble. What more can be said?* And then I read the following teaching from Rav Ashlag.

Moses was the scribe of the Torah, and the Creator told him what to write. In the portion of Beha'alotcha, the Creator came to Moses and told to him to write down the words *Veha ish Moshe* (" And the man Moses"), and Moses dipped the *kulmus*, the writing instrument, into the ink, wondering whether God would now add something negative about him. The Creator told Moses to write the word *anav*, which means "humble."

The question the kabbalists famously ask is this: The Hebrew word *anav*, or humble, is written with four letters, *Ayin*, *Nun*, *Yud*, *Vav*, so why is it written as *Ayin*, *Nun*, *Vav* in the Torah?

The *Midrash* says that the ink used to inscribe the Torah was miraculous and that Moses was given exactly the right amount needed to write the letters and words of the Torah. So what happened to the ink that should have been used for the missing *Yud*?

Rav Ashlag explains that Moses was so overwhelmed from writing such congratulatory words about himself that his hands shook when he wrote as the Creator commanded. In his shaking, Moses spilled the ink that was meant to write the letter *Yud*.

The *Midrash* explains that this drop of ink was not wasted or lost. It is this ink that makes the face of Moses shine with such tremendous Light, prompting the biblical line in Exodus: "When Aaron and all the Israelites saw Moses, his face was radiant, and they were afraid to come near him." (Exodus 34:35)

The beauty of the gift of humility is that it's available to all of us. Anyone can be humble. But paradoxically, true humility is perhaps the most difficult thing in the world to achieve, which is what makes the insights of the portion of Beha'alotcha so valuable.

SHLACH LECHA

The Bible says: "And the Lord spoke to Moses saying, 'Send men, that they may spy out the land of Canaan, which I give to the children of Israel; of every tribe of their fathers shall you send a man, everyone a prince among them.'" (Numbers 13:1-2) In this portion, Moses was told to *schlach*, or "send out," a scout from each of the twelve tribes. He did so, and when the spies returned, they reported all kinds of obstacles, including fierce enemies, which frightened the Israelites. The negativity of the twelve scouts resulted in the death of most of them, as well as the effect of wandering forty more years in the desert before they could enter the land of Canaan.

To avoid making this same mistake in our own lives, we need to understand where the scouts went wrong. In discussing the portion of Shlach Lecha, Rabbi Moshe ben Nachman of Girondi, also known as Nachmanides, asks a very practical question: "If Moses told the spies to look at the land and to see what type of people were living there, and the spies did so, answering his questions truthfully when they came back, then what did they do wrong? Did Moses want them to come back and lie to him? He had asked them to spy out the land, and they did so. What was wrong with that?"

The first important understanding we can take from this biblical story is the danger of being right. Even when we have been awakened spiritually through a connection to the Light of the Creator, there will still be times when we are wrong. The trickiest time of all, however—the time when we are in the gravest spiritual danger—comes when we are right. Everything the spies said was accurate, according to their point of view. But what they forgot in their rightness was to leave an opening for the Light of the Creator.

Recently, a married couple came to see me. They had come to the point in their relationship where they realized they both needed to make changes for their marriage to work. For a long time, the wife had believed that she had no need to change because she was always right. But now she was seeing that being right, whether she was or not, was putting her relationship with her husband in jeopardy. This is true for all of us, and it is especially true spiritually. More often than not, when we think we are right, we are wrong, but paradoxically, the spiritual fallout from being right is far more damaging than the damage that can result from being wrong.

Rabbi Levi Yitzchak of Berditchev, the *Kedushat Levi*, says that when the twelve men selected by Moses believed their job was to go into Canaan and spy out the land and the people living there, they were ignoring the spiritual side of things—the deeper forces at work in the world. The Creator had really sent them into Canaan so that they could pray, study, and do spiritual work, awakening Light from the Upper Worlds to flow down into the land itself. They were to awaken a desire in the land itself for the Israelites to come to the land, making their entry peaceful and harmonious.

The *Kedushat Levi* points out the disconnect between what the spies thought their job was and the job itself. On the physical level, they were right, but their job had a deeper spiritual dimension, which they neglected. Because the spies thought they were right, their minds closed to other possibilities and they got it wrong. The kabbalists teach us that the current exile that we are all living through tracks back to this mistake.

The portion of Shlach Lecha awakens in us an awareness that whatever we consider our job in this world may have nothing to do with our true mission. Moreover, if we allow ourselves to become identified with what we think we are meant to do—if we decide that we're right—it will take us longer to figure out the truth, and in the meantime, we could be getting things badly wrong.

If we could have gone to the scouts while they were spending their forty days in the land of Canaan and had asked them, "Why are you in such a rush? Don't you think you should take time to reveal Light through your morning prayers?" They might have answered, "Yes, it may be important to reveal Light every morning, but God and Moses sent us here for an even more important job. We have to spy out the land and its people. We can't waste too much time praying or studying because our job is to gather information on the richness of the land and the strength of its inhabitants." How terribly misguided even the princes among us can be!

From the perspective provided by the *Kedushat Levi*, the scouts seem almost ridiculous. By focusing on the letter of their mission, they missed its spirit. And today, we are all still paying for this mistake.

We are also still falling into the same trap. When we wake up with our egos all wrapped up in whatever we think we are supposed to be doing today, we are behaving like the Israelite scouts. When we rigidly stick to our plan, regardless of its spiritual content, we are also behaving like those spies. Every time we let spiritual work give way to being right, we perpetuate darkness and exile. By being open to the idea that what we think we are supposed to be doing today may not be what the Creator wants for us, we prepare ourselves to reveal Light. The only way to avoid the trap of the Israelite scouts is to disregard our plans, to disregard our logic, and to let the Creator show us the way.

According to recently discovered writings by Rav Ashlag, when the Creator sees that someone is simple in their connection to the Light and that they do not have great plans for themselves, the secrets and Light of the Creator flow more easily through them.

Rabbi Naftali of Ropshitz, the *Zera Kodesh*, who was born on the same day the Baal Shem Tov passed away, was a very famous kabbalist and student of Rav Elimelech of Lizhensk. The *Zera Kodesh* says that when the scouts believed that they knew what their work was and thus fell spiritually, they also lost their only hope to awaken true humility. Humility is what gives us the ability to let go of our plans and our logic. If we had absolute humility, we would have no plans or logic.

The *Zera Kodesh* asks why, in the portion of Shlach Lecha, the land of Israel is referred to as the land of Canaan. Indeed, this is not often the case in the Bible. The *Zera Kodesh* explains that the gift of both the spiritual and physical land of Israel is to awaken this level of humility. In Hebrew, the word "Canaan," *Kena'an*, is similar to the word *lehikana'a*, which means "to surrender." So Moses told the spies then—and is telling us now—that on this Shabbat, we need to enter the land of humility and we need to surrender. As the *Zera Kodesh* explains: "Those who merit entering into the spiritual land of Israel are those who, even if they have achieved something, view themselves as small."

According to the *Zera Kodesh*, the death of the spies and the forty years the Israelites spent in the desert were not so much a punishment as they were a matter of cause and effect. If our life's focus is not on the Supernal, if it is not on humility, we will not be granted entry into the land, which is the Tree of Life. This exile and this darkness is not a punishment; it is simply a result of our actions, of cause and effect.

Rabbi Yonatan ben Uziel, who translated the Torah into Aramaic and provided his own commentary, says that in this portion, Moses is counting the twelve spies when suddenly, as if out of nowhere, the Bible says that Moses gave Hoshea the name Joshua by adding the letter *Yud*. Why? According to Yonatan ben Uziel, Moses saw that one man of the twelve scouts was truly humble, and it was to this man that Moses gave a new name as a prayer and a blessing. The *Yud* added to Hoshea's name connected him to the Light of the Creator and thus protected him from making the same mistake as the other spies.

But why was this prayer of Moses directed at Joshua alone? Did Moses not care for the other eleven spies? We know that Caleb did not fall either, so why did Moses not also pray for Caleb? The answer is that blessings cannot be given to a person who is not working to kill his ego. When Moses saw that the other eleven spies were not doing so, he understood that there was no use in praying for them. Humility is truly what the portion of Shlach Lecha has to awaken within us. When we arise every morning, instead of thinking, *How I can make myself wiser?* or even *How I can help people more?* we can ask ourselves this: "What can I do to make myself more humble today?"

According to the kabbalists, the Creator promises that whoever has humility will finish their correction in this incarnation. Humility is a phenomenal spiritual booster, like the Counting of the Omer, and humility is available to use all year round, if only we recognize its power. We can study, pray, and meditate all day. We can help other people throughout our entire lifetime, but still this will not be enough. If, however, we achieve humility, the Creator promises that we will finish our correction right now, in this lifetime.

The *Arvei Nachal* says that prayers that contain ego cannot be heard by the Creator. Because these prayers cannot enter the Supernal Worlds they remain stuck in this world. So what do we do? All of us have egos. The *Midrash* and the kabbalists tell us the very act of trying to minimize our egos creates hope. When we make an effort to learn from the story of the twelve spies in Shlach Lecha, we awaken ourselves to the truth that the only way to enter the land of Israel—*Etz HaChaim*, the Tree of Life—is to replace our desire to be right with humility. This way, we make room for spirit. This way, we merit blessings, assistance, and prayers.

KORACH

The thirty-eighth portion of the Torah begins: "Now Korach, the son of Izhar, the son of Kehath, the son of Levi, with Dathan and Abiram, the sons of Eliab and On, the son of Peleth, sons of Reuben, took men; and they rose up in the face of Moses, with certain of the Children of Israel, two hundred and fifty men; they were princes of the congregation, the elect men of the assembly, men of renown; and they assembled themselves together against Moses and against Aaron, and said to them, 'You take too much upon yourselves, seeing all the congregation are holy, every one of them, and God is among them; why do you then lift yourselves up above the assembly of God?' And when Moses heard it, he fell upon his face."

For the most part, the early commentators have judged Korach harshly. For a long time, scholars have accepted the general understanding that Korach wanted to become High Priest and challenged Moses and Aaron for the position. Taken literally, this story casts Moses and Aaron in a good light, and Korach as a bad actor, which is why, in the end, Korach and those around him were swallowed up by the earth. The *Gemara* discusses whether or not Korach's soul has any hope of correction, and there are even those who say that although all the other souls of humanity will be resurrected, the soul of Korach never will.

In the commentaries of the later kabbalists, especially those of the Ari and the students of the Baal Shem Tov, we begin to see a different Korach emerge. One of the first questions this raises is how we should view the Torah. If its words don't change, how can what we learn from it be so variable? The *Zohar* makes it clear that the stories in the Torah are just its shell and that this outer covering has many layers, while Rav Ashlag tells us that the Creator is hidden within the Torah and that the spiritual work of humanity is to reveal His hidden Light.

Rabbi Zev Wolf of Zotamir, also known as the *Ohr HaMeir*, explains that when we interact with the Torah, we create what the kabbalists call *tzerufim*, or arrangements of the letters of the Torah as they pertain to our lives. He says that the purpose of this lifetime is really *tzerufei HaTorah*, to make a new Torah as we connect to the Light of the Creator. How do we do this? The *Ohr HaMeir* explains that we use the letters of the Torah all the time; we speak with the essence of the letters of the Torah whenever we discuss anything that gives us sustenance and life. And through the lives we lead, we create different combinations of the letters of the Torah.

The *Ohr HaMeir* quotes Maimonides, also known as the Rambam, as saying that although the essence of the Torah existed before the time of Creation, the stories were created later. But how can the Torah have existed before the time of Creation if the stories of

Abraham, Isaac, and Jacob, for example, occur afterwards? The Rambam explains that the essence of the Torah—all the Names of the Creator—consists of different combinations of the same letters that we have in the written Torah. When, for instance, Abraham went through the process of the Binding of Isaac, his life created a different combination of the letters from that which had existed previously, thus leading to the words that we read today as the story of the Binding of Isaac.

So the first time the Torah existed, it did not contain any stories. It had the letters we know, but only in combinations of the Name of the Creator. The lives of the *tzadikim*—righteous people like Abraham, Isaac, Jacob, and Moses—created new combinations of those letters, which are what we see in the present form of the Torah today. This process continues, so that although the essence of the Torah never changes, the *tzerufim*, or arrangements of the letters of the Torah, do.

The great chariots—Abraham, Isaac, Jacob, and Moses—created stable and strong *tzerufim*, but we ourselves still change the Torah with our conduct today. For example, the spiritual work we have done prior to the Shabbat of Korach influences what *tzerufim*—what understandings or what levels of vision—we will get from this particular Torah portion when we connect with it on Shabbat. Hopefully, the Korach we read about this year is different from the Korach we read about last year because we are different this year.

The *Ohr HaMeir* continues: "Every week, the letters of the Torah wait for us; the portion waits to create new combinations of the existing letters based on the work we've done that week. Every day of our lives, we rewrite our own Torah: When we commit negative deeds, we write bad stories; when we take positive action, the stories are good." If we read the portion of Korach today and see his story as negative, it is only because we ourselves are negative. But when the Messiah comes, the Torah will be revealed to us in its true essence, and then there will be no negative stories, only positive ones.

Every day of our lives, we do one of two things: We create positive combinations of the letters of the Torah, or we take those letters that are meant to be combined in positive ways and we put them it into the darkness, into negativity. We need to constantly hold onto this understanding because it is very important to remember in our study and in our work. If we truly accept responsibility for the *tzerufim* (the combinations of the letters within the Torah), then we will appreciate the spiritual importance of the lives we lead.

Hopefully, our goal on the Shabbat of Korach is to make a strong connection to Korach because as we begin to understand what he did and why, the Korach of today can assist us in our own spiritual development. The Ari explains that the last letters of three words from Psalms 92:13, *tzadi**k** ketama**r** yifra**ch*** ("the righteous shall flourish"), which we sing every Friday night, spell the word "Korach." The Ari asks why we would want to connect to these words every Friday evening if we didn't see Korach as having the ability to achieve righteousness. Korach was an important soul who did something so difficult that most of us would be unwilling to take it on.

Rabbi Yitzchak Isaac of Komarno, the *Heichal HaBrachah*, explains that Korach wanted to bring about the Final Redemption right away. This was his strongest desire. But the time was not yet right because the negative side held lots of sparks of Light captive, it was still strong. If the Israelites had not fallen spiritually by worshiping the golden calf, they could have triggered the time of the Messiah, but they were not ready. There was still too much power left on the negative side, and therefore, Korach did not succeed.

When we see Korach in this new light, everything changes. The Bible says: "When Moses heard what Korach and his friends wanted to do, he fell on his face." Many commentators say that Moses fell out of embarrassment because he was so upset by what was happening. But the father of the *Esh Kodesh*, Rav Elimelech Shapira of Grodzhisk, the *Imrei Elimelech*, says that Moses fell on his face because he was trying to help Korach elevate the sparks trapped in the negative side.

The *Talmud* explains that there are great souls, like Korach, who are willing to risk everything to give the world a chance to achieve the *Gemar HaTikkun* (Final Correction). Even if, having sacrificed everything, they won't be able to be there when the *Gemar HaTikkun* comes, they are still willing to take that chance. The Ari says that there is a prayer called *Nefilat Hapayim*, where a person falls on his or her face; the purpose of this prayer is to free and elevate the sparks of Light captured by the negative side. Moses performed the *Nefilat Hapayim* prayer to elevate some more sparks from the negative side, thereby giving Korach and his friends a greater chance to succeed.

The *Heichal HaBrachah* says that Korach wanted to correct both the sin of Adam and the sin of the golden calf by elevating all the souls that had fallen into darkness, thereby bringing about the Final Redemption. But he overlooked something. Korach was so intent on sacrificing everything for his goal that he forgot to awaken the appropriate level of love for Moses. Korach had some feeling of this kind for Moses, but not enough. When Moses told Korach that he didn't think he would succeed and therefore not to go forward,

Korach should have surrendered to Moses' judgment out of love. If Korach had done so, the *Heichal HaBrachah* tells us that Korach and his assembly would have succeeded in bringing about the *Gemar HaTikkun* right then and there.

Very few people throughout history have been willing act as Korach did. How many of us would be willing to give up everything for just a slim chance of ending pain, suffering, and death in this world? Although we may not be meant to sacrifice like Korach did, we do need to be moving our spiritual process in that direction. On the Shabbat that bears his name, Korach assists us in reawakening a tremendous desire for the strength to sacrifice for the *Gemar HaTikkun*. We don't know exactly where Korach is now, but we do know that throughout the generations, his soul has been elevating. And because we are drawing near to the *Gemar HaTikkun*, chances are good that Korach has elevated very high indeed.

The Ari tells a very famous story about a great *tzadik* who lived in Galilee about five hundred years ago. Like Korach, Joseph de la Reina was willing to bring about the Final Redemption in his time. So he gathered his closest students and told them to go bid their wives and children goodbye, for there was a good chance they would not see them again. Then de la Reina and his students went to visit the grave of Rav Shimon bar Yochai in Meron, where they fasted and read from the *Zohar*. When Rav Shimon bar Yochai revealed himself to Joseph de la Reina and his students, they asked him to bless their attempt to bring about the Redemption. But Rav Shimon told them, "I know how great your souls are. I know how elevated you are, but the chances of your succeeding are so slim that I cannot give you my blessing."

Still, Joseph de la Reina and his students continued in their endeavor. They went into the desert to fast, pray, and study, this time asking for the soul of Elijah the Prophet to be revealed to them. When their request was granted, they asked Elijah to help them, but he, too, replied, "I ask you not to continue, for the world is not ready. There is still too much strength in the negative side. If you try now, you're going to fail."

Joseph de la Reina and his students all agreed to go ahead with their mission. This story ends with the *Samech-Mem* (the Negative Angel) overtaking them. Some of the students died right away. Others lost their minds. Joseph de la Reina remained alive for some time, but like Korach, he eventually fell to the depths. In his book *Gate of Reincarnation*, the Ari describes the different incarnations that Joseph de la Reina had to live through during the process of his correction.

The Bible says that after Korach failed in his attempt to bring about the *Geulah*, or Redemption, the earth swallowed him up. Rabbi Elimelech of Lizhensk, the *Noam Elimelech*, interprets this by saying, "Korach had the aspect of the soul of Cain in him, which is why he was swallowed up by the earth. The death of Korach was actually a correction of the killing of Abel."

Before we pick up on this provocative idea, I'd like to digress for a moment to share with you a fascinating perspective on Cain that I heard recently. According to this teaching, Cain did not know that such a thing as death existed. He knew that he was alive and that so were his parents, Adam and Eve, and his brother, Abel. But no one he knew had ever died, so when he got upset and hit his brother, Abel, there was no thought in Cain's mind that Abel was dead. So after Cain saw Abel fall, he waited, expecting Abel to pick himself up. The *Midrash* says that Cain sat next to Abel for days, crying and begging his brother to arise.

The *Noam Elimelech*'s interpretation of Korach's death as a correction for the first murder in the history of the world gives us an even broader perspective from which to view the story of Korach and Moses. In order for Cain, whose soul reincarnated as Korach, to correct his soul, he needed to be killed somehow by Abel, whose soul reincarnated as Moses. The *Noam Elimelech* says we should forget everything we have learned about Korach up to now because the portion of Korach is really a form of misdirection. The deeper truth is that Korach's life had to end the way it did in order to correct what he did to his brother, Abel.

So with our new understanding of the story of Korach, it becomes clear that this is not just the story of Korach and Moses; it is an account of the correction of Cain for killing Abel. This is not a negative story, for Cain/Korach *needed* this correction. When we look at our own lives from this perspective, we begin to have more appreciation for who we are and what we are going through. We may think our personal story is only as old as the number of years we have spent in this lifetime, but this is not the case. Who knows how many incarnations and experiences our soul has been through just to be here at this moment?

What we do know is that whatever correction we may be going through is necessary—not just to correct the events of this lifetime, but also to correct events that may have taken place hundreds or thousands of years ago. When we begin to see the story of Korach and Moses in this spiritual context, we begin to see our own life, and the people in it, from this perspective as well.

CHUKAT

When kabbalists discuss the portion of Chukat, they refer to a concept called *Amarti achakmah vehi rechokah mimeni*, meaning that there is something very difficult to comprehend about the portion of Chukat. According to the *Zohar*, when King Solomon said, "All this have I proved by wisdom: I said, I will be wise; but it was far from me," he was speaking about the portion of Chukat. This is a difficult portion to unpack for its meaning, according even to the wisest of sages.

Chukat or "statute" begins with a detailed description of the Creator's rules for the red-heifer ceremony needed to provide purification for those who have had contact with a dead body. "This is the ordinance of the law [*Zot chukat haTorah*] which God has commanded, saying, 'Speak to the children of Israel that they bring you a red heifer without spot, wherein there is no blemish, and upon which never came a yoke.'" The commentators explain that *zot chukat haTorah* means "this is something that you won't explain," and the sages tell us that with these words, the Creator was really coming to Moses and saying, "I am going to give you something called *chukat haTorah*, which I will not reveal to anyone but you."

So what is this revelation that the Creator would share only with Moses? We know that it must somehow include the core aspects of this portion, the first of which is the process of the *para aduma*, the red heifer, which involves purification from *tum'at met*, the negative energy from a dead body. The other key to this portion is the miraculous story of Moses striking the rock to replace the loss of the well of Miriam.

The *Midrash* says in the portion just prior to Chukat, that when Korach and his friends rose up against Moses, they accused him of many things, including sexual betrayal. They accused Moses of cuckolding them, giving many Israelites the impression that Moses may have been sleeping with their wives. According to the kabbalists, the secret revelation that the Creator chose to give Moses was in recognition of not only all the spiritual work Moses had done while he was leading the Israelites, but also of the humiliation he would suffer as a result of Korach's accusations.

On the Shabbat of Chukat, the Creator gave Moses *bila hamavet lanetzach*, the energy of dominion over death, the key to removing *tum'at met*, the negative energy neutralized by the sacrifice of the red heifer. This great gift was not a transmission of information, but of consciousness. As the Rav often says, "The only barrier between where we are today and *bila hamavet lanetzach*—the removal of pain, suffering, and death completely from our world—is our consciousness." Because Moses had the consciousness of clarity and certainty that death *can* be removed, death *was* removed from him. The *Midrash* says that no one knows where Moses is buried, and the

Zohar explains that this is because Moses never was buried. Like Elijah the Prophet, he achieved immortality.

When Moses was graced with the gift of immortality, he told the Creator that he could not accept being the only one of his generation to possess this consciousness. So the Creator said, "We will give the Israelites a chance to join you. Tell them that the well of Miriam is leaving them and will be replaced when you ask a rock to give them water, and see what their response is. If they hold even a shadow of doubt that words can change the natural course of things, then they are not ready for this consciousness I have given you."

The *Midrash* vividly describes the miracle that took place when Moses took the Israelites to the rock. Although there were hundreds and thousands of Israelites present, when they came to the rock, each of them saw him- or herself standing alone in front of it, with no one else around. The *Midrash* explains that if even just one of them had possessed the certainty that Moses could draw water from the rock, immortality would have occurred for them as it did for Moses. But no one did.

The Bible says that instead of speaking to the rock, Moses struck it with his staff. Water did pour from the rock and the Israelites were able to drink, but the Bible says that Moses was punished for not doing exactly as the Creator had instructed him. Moses' punishment was that he and Aaron would not be allowed to enter the land of Israel with the Israelites. But Rav Ashlag explains that Moses not entering the land of Israel was not a matter of punishment, for Moses didn't make a mistake. Instead, he and the Creator saw that the Israelites were not ready. This was why the Creator told Moses, "You will have to leave them before they reach Israel, Moses, and come back in every generation to see if they are ready for immortality."

The *Midrash* says that Moses' soul does come back in every generation to see if we are ready to receive the gift of life without death. Each time, the answer is no, and Moses goes away, only to return in the following generation. This year, on the Shabbat of Chukat, we need to ask ourselves whether *we* truly believe that pain, suffering, and death can be removed from our world. And if we don't, then we need to beg the Creator for this consciousness.

According to Kabbalah, in order for us to gain the consciousness of immortality, we have to first understand that any sadness we feel in our lives comes from *tum'at met*, the energy of death, and that until we achieve clarity about the cause of this sadness, we cannot remove it from our lives. We bring the energy of death into our lives when we act from our ego. The negative side wants to convince us that there are other reasons for our sadness and our disappointment, but we need to realize that they have only one cause: the Desire to Receive for the Self Alone. When we attain this clarity, we can begin the work of removing sadness and disappointment from our lives forever.

The commentators on the Torah tell us that the discussion of the removal of *tum'at met*, the removal of the energy of death, does not belong in the portion of Chukat at all. The portion of Chukat focuses on what occurred in the fortieth year of the Israelites' journey in the desert, whereas the revelation of the red heifer and the removal of *tum'at met* took place many years earlier, in the second year after the Israelites' exodus from Egypt. So why is the discussion of the red heifer, *chukat haTorah*, revealed in Chukat, when Miriam and Aaron pass away, and not when it actually happened?

The answer is that Moses could not have received the level of consciousness of going beyond the unclean energy of death, had it not been for the embarrassment and pain caused to him by Korach.

This is why the story of Moses receiving *chukat haTorah* is where it is. Although this level of consciousness was described by the Creator earlier in the Bible, if not for Korach and his contribution to the diminishment of whatever ego was left in Moses, Moses could not have achieved the consciousness of "his burial place is not known."

There is a story about the great kabbalist, Rav Chaim Hezekiah Medini, the *Sedei Chemed*, who lived in Hebron more than a hundred years ago. He was widely beloved as a wise man and a scholar, but there was one man in Hebron who was very jealous of this great kabbalist. This man came up with a wicked scheme to dishonor the *Sedei Chemed*. He arranged for the cleaning lady of the synagogue where the *Sedei Chemed* went to pray to accuse the *Sedei Chemed* of trying to rape her.

The very next morning, while the *Sedei Chemed* sat and studied, the cleaning lady ran out of the building as everyone was entering to pray, her clothing disheveled, screaming that the *Sedei Chemed* had attacked her! Fortunately, everyone knew the charge was ludicrous, so the woman was fired from her job.

Years went by. Then one day, the woman came to the *Sedei Chemed* and said, "I'm terribly sorry for what I did to you a number of years ago, but the man who asked me to do this promised to support me and my family. He has done so all this time, but now he has passed away, and I have no way to put food on the table. Although most people believed that you couldn't have done such a thing, I am sure that even to this day, there are some who have their doubts. If you wish, I will go before the entire community and tell them that I was lying, but please, can you help me find a job? Can you help me feed my family?"

After listening to this woman's apology and her plea, the *Sedei Chemed* took her to a student of his and asked him to take her into his employ. Once again, the woman volunteered to stand before everyone and tell the truth about what had happened years before, but the *Sedei Chemed* replied, "I'm asking you not to do that. Let me explain why. When you ran out yelling that I had raped you, I was terribly embarrassed, of course. But because of this embarrassment, my ego was nearly annihilated, and all the Gates of Wisdom opened up for me. Now I'm afraid that if you withdraw this accusation, those gates might close up again."

The *Sedei Chemed* suffered terrible embarrassment. Moses fell on his face. But what happened next for them? For the *Sedei Chemed*, it was the opening of all the Gates of Wisdom. For Moses, it was immortality. The Shabbat of Chukat is the Shabbat of the removal of the energy of death. To receive this gift, however, first we need understand that embarrassment is a valuable tool for diminishing our ego and gaining entry into the *Etz HaChaim* (Tree of Life) reality. Secondly, we need to know that we alone are the sole cause of sadness in our lives. When we take these two understandings and beg for Moses to give us the consciousness of *chukat haTorah*, the consciousness of the removal of *tum'at met*, we truly create a great change.

BALAK

In the portion of Balak, the Bible tells us that Bilaam the prophet had the power to cast a curse on the Israelites, to give them the evil eye. The *Zohar* says: "The eye of Bilaam the wicked was evil in every way. Anywhere he gazed was destroyed as with a flame, since there does not exist such an evil eye in the world as the eye of the wicked one." In our previous discussion of Korach, we came to realize that early kabbalistic commentaries portrayed a very different Korach from the later commentaries because the journey of Korach's soul continued beyond his physical death. As we tracked his progress, Korach went from villain to *tzadik*. Can we do the same with Bilaam?

As I considered this, I remembered a study session with my father, the Rav, and my brother, Yehuda, more than twenty-five years ago. The Rav often studied from the *Kitvei HaAri*, the writings of Rabbi Isaac Luria, the Ari, and Yehuda, and I would join him every night to study. In one of our study sessions, the Ari revealed to us the spiritual journey of the soul of Bilaam.

According to the Bible, once Balak, the king of Moab, saw how successful the Israelites were in battle, he became afraid, so he called on Bilaam to put a curse on the Israelites. But God intervened, putting His own words into Bilaam's mouth so that instead of cursing the Israelites, Bilaam praised them, saying, "Who can count the dust of Jacob, and the number of the fourth part of Israel? Let me die the death of the righteous, and let my last end be like his!"

The Ari says that it is very difficult to understand this statement in light of the fact that Bilaam did *not* die the death of the righteous. The *Zohar* tells us that Bilaam's death was a death of impurity; when Pinchas killed Bilaam, he used a sword that had on it the image of a snake, a symbol of idol worship, to ensure that Bilaam did not die the death of the righteous. So why would Bilaam, speaking with words the Creator put in his mouth, ask to die the death of the righteous and then not do so?

The Ari explains that there is a very important spiritual principle at work here: reincarnation, the ability of souls to go through many lifetimes in order to make their corrections. The reason for Bilaam not dying the positive death of a righteous person is linked to the fact that the soul of Bilaam was reincarnated in Naval HaKarmeli, a wealthy man who lived at the time of King David. But before we get into the story of Naval HaKarmeli, how do we know that the Ari is right in making this claim?

We find some persuasive evidence in the observations of a student of the Ari, the great kabbalist Rav Chaim Vital: "Very often, I would be walking in the field with my teacher, the Ari, and he would point to a rock or a bush and say the name of a person to me. My teacher would then explain that because of a certain negative action that this person had done in his life, his soul was now in that rock or in that bush. And these were people whom the Ari, my teacher, never knew." Rav Chaim Vital would return home after these walks in the fields with his teacher and ask around town about the people that the Ari had just mentioned to him. It was not that he didn't trust his teacher, but he was curious to see if his teacher was right. Rav Chaim Vital says, "And we found, time after time, that everything my teacher said about these people, whom he had never met but whose souls he saw in the rocks and in the bushes, was true."

The Ari himself says that the fact that people can be reincarnated into inanimate objects can be seen with the soul of Bilaam. The soul of Bilaam was first incarnated as Lavan Ha'Arami, the father-in-law of Jacob, who was a negative person. Next came its incarnation as Bilaam the prophet, who had the power to curse the Israelites. Then, the Ari explains, Bilaam's soul was reincarnated as a rock because Bilaam had used his mouth negatively, and as a stone, he could not speak. The soul of Bilaam's next incarnation after that was as Naval HaKarmeli, a wealthy man who lived at the time of King David, and in this incarnation, Bilaam's soul was given an opportunity to complete its *tikkun*, or correction, in this case of evil speech.

According to the Book of Prophets, King David, seemingly out of the blue, sent a group of soldiers to Naval HaKarmeli with a request. King David said, "Tell Naval that when his people were traveling with their herds, I and my soldiers protected him, and because of this protection, I now ask that Naval provide us with food and drink so we can sustain ourselves." The Ari reminds us that there were many other people of whom King David could have made this request, but he sent his messengers to Naval. What did Naval do once he received King David's request? Naval denied his request. Although he knew King David, he said, "Who is David? Who is this son of Ishai? There is no way I'm going to help him."

Abigail, Naval's wife, overheard this conversation and realized that her husband was making a terrible mistake. Without telling him, she ran after the soldiers and stopped them, giving them food and drink, and promising more to King David. But she was too late. Shortly after denying King David's request, Naval died. According to the phrase in the Book of Prophets, "his heart died within him."

The Ari explains that Naval was an elevated soul whose *tikkun* process had begun much earlier, first in his soul's incarnation as Lavan, and then as Bilaam. When Pinchas killed Bilaam, he was actually assisting in the correction of Bilaam's soul. The Ari says that Bilaam was then reincarnated into a stone, which could not speak, to give Bilaam's soul the opportunity to begin the correction of his evil mouth. This would make it possible for Bilaam's soul to reincarnate as Naval HaKarmeli.

His incarnation as Naval HaKarmeli was the first time since incarnating as a stone that Bilaam's soul took human form as part of his process of correction. King David was not simply sending his soldiers to some random person; King David knew that Naval had incarnated to correct the evil speech of Bilaam, so he sent messengers to give Bilaam/Naval a chance to purify his mouth. But unfortunately, Naval still was unable to control his tongue.

But what happened next? The Ari says that Naval had a vision of his spiritual process, in which everything was suddenly revealed to him. Naval realized that he was the incarnation of Lavan and Bilaam. He also realized that because he had used his mouth negatively he had been reincarnated into a stone and that now, with the help of King David, he had been given a chance to correct his evil speech, but he had failed. He was so upset that he had missed the opportunity for his correction that his heart died within him and, as the Book of Prophets says, "he made himself into a stone."

When we look at this story literally, Naval does not seem like a very good person, but when we take a step back, we begin to see the greatness of this soul. The Ari tells us he was a great soul in Lavan, and in Bilaam, as well as in the stone, and then in Naval. After falling spiritually by speaking badly of King David, Naval realized what he had done and took the next step in his correction. And although Naval had not yet completed that correction, the Ari tells us that Naval died *motye sharim*, the death of righteousness, fulfilling the prophecy of Bilaam.

The Ari tells us that after Naval, the next incarnation of Bilaam's soul was as Barzilai HaGiladi. As he was dying on his deathbed, King David told his son, King Solomon, "But show kindness to the sons of Barzilai HaGiladi, and let them be of those that eat at your table." Why? Barzilai HaGiladi had sustained King David and his soldiers where Naval had not, but this was not the real reason. The Ari reveals that King David knew that Barzilai HaGiladi was actually the incarnation of the soul of Naval and of Lavan and of Bilaam, and that what this soul did not correct in its incarnation as Naval, it would continue to work on during its incarnation as Barzilai. Barzilai HaGiladi's death was also the death of the righteous, and by the time Bilaam's soul was incarnated into the son of Barzilai HaGiladi, he was completely corrected.

With the benefit of this larger perspective, we can see what a mistake it would be to judge Bilaam as evil. No one's soul is ever static. Once we might have looked at the lives of Lavan, Bilaam, and Naval HaKarmeli, and thought how terrible they were. But now we see that their lives were growing in virtue all along. Lavan became a better person when his soul became Bilaam; Bilaam continued that transformation when his soul entered a stone and then Naval; Naval did the same when his soul was reborn as Barzilai; and when Barzilai incarnated as his own son, he was now a completely righteous and corrected soul.

This is a valuable lesson for our own lives. There is never any spiritual falling without redemption. No soul falls forever. With deeper insight, we realize that every soul, no matter how low it might seem, is in a process of correction.

There is a verse of Isaiah, which says: "Look around and see; they have gathered and come to surround you." The Ari tells us this verse is describing the *Gemar HaTikkun*, the Final Correction, and that the first three letters of the words ***n**ikbatzu **b**a'u **l**echa* ("have gathered and come to surround you") make up the name "Naval." When we "look around," we awaken the consciousness that no soul truly falls—it is simply in a process of correction; when we "look around," we see all the souls are here; when we "look around and see" the past, the present, and the future, we realize that Bilaam is a *tzadik*.

The Ari says it is important for us to study this teaching because it awakens us to the understanding that there are no negative souls; that no one is falling. All souls are righteous, and we are all in the process of correction. Even when we see something as negative, we must remember that there is tremendous holiness within it. We need to read these words over and over again in order to awaken this consciousness within us so that we may move toward the *Gemar HaTikkun*.

If we read the portion of Balak and see Bilaam as a negative person, it turns out that we are connecting to something that doesn't even exist anymore. Barzilai HaGiladi and the son of Barzilai HaGiladi lived many, many years ago, which means that Bilaam became a *tzadik* long before we even began our current correction. On this Shabbat of Balak, we are meeting the righteous Bilaam. On this Shabbat, we start seeing holiness and righteousness around us all the time.

In the Introduction to the *Ten Luminous Emanations*, Rav Ashlag says that when a person corrects his negativity, his negative actions also turn into Light. We are all on a path of correction, and when we look back at some of the things we have done, we may feel embarrassed. But if we never fell, the amount of Light revealed through our work would be far smaller. There is no reason for embarrassment or shame when we consider our past mistakes. On the contrary, everything that we did wrong yesterday makes this Light today—as we work on our correction—shine even brighter. Another gift we receive on the Shabbat of Balak is that when we are on the right path, we need to acknowledge all of our darkness. We need to maintain the memory of all the times we have stumbled and fallen spiritually because this awareness beautifies, strengthens, and elevates everything we do now.

PINCHAS

The portion of Balak concludes with the story of a man and a woman who committed a sexual act in public, but does not mention their names. The Israelites were already suffering from a terrible plague brought upon them by the Creator, angered by their "harlotry with the daughters of Moab" and their "sacrifices of their gods." To stop the plague, Pinchas took a spear and ran it through the man and the woman, but not before 24,000 people had lost their lives.

In the portion of Pinchas, as if out of nowhere, the Bible gives us the names of the two sinners: Kozbi, the daughter of Tzur, a princess of Midian, and Zimri ben Salu, a leader of the tribe of Shimon. The *Arvei Nachal* says that by mentioning their names, the Torah is signaling that the spiritual correction of these two souls has begun. Now that we have learned about the righteousness of Korach and of Bilaam, it will come as no surprise to hear that Kozbi and Zimri are also incredible souls. Although Pinchas is the central *tzadik* of this portion that bears his name, the correction of the souls of Kozbi and Zimri will be our focus, for it provides us with some unusual lessons.

As we've seen, to understand the significance of a story, we always need to take a step back. The kabbalists reveal that the souls of Kozbi and Zimri had previously been incarnated as Dina and Shechem; Dina was the daughter that Jacob hid from his brother and who was later raped by Shechem. Unfortunately, when two souls are locked in battle, they continue to make each other fall. This was true of Dina and Shechem, so when their souls came back as Kozbi and Zimri, they brought each other down once again. They could have continued to fall, but something happened—Pinchas happened.

After Kozbi was killed by Pinchas' spear, her soul incarnated as Jezebel, wife of one of the kings at the time of Elijah the Prophet. In the Haftarah of the portion of Pinchas, we read how Jezebel caused trouble for Elijah the Prophet all of his life, and now we understand why. Pinchas' soul had reincarnated as Elijah the Prophet, and Jezebel remembered the pain she had suffered at Pinchas' hands during her soul's earlier incarnation as Kozbi.

In his book *Chesed LeAvraham*, Rabbi Avraham Azulai tells us that the soul of Zimri ben Salu, the man who was slain by Pinchas, would later reincarnate as the great kabbalist Rabbi Akiva. As an illustration of just how elevated Rabbi Akiva was, the *Midrash* tells us that when Moses went up to the Heavens to receive the Torah, he saw the soul of Rabbi Akiva and said to the Creator, "This soul is greater than mine. Here is the person who should reveal this great Light in the world, not me." To which the Creator replied, "I will decide who reveals this Light to the world."

The question is how could Moses be looking at the soul of Rabbi Akiva? Rabbi Akiva had not been born yet; his soul was currently in Zimri ben Salu from the tribe of Shimon. So how did Moses see the soul of Rabbi Akiva—the corrected Zimri ben Salu—when Zimri was alive and falling spiritually in this world?

The truth is that Rabbi Akiva has always existed. In one incarnation, he was Shechem, a rapist; and in another, he was Zimri, a man who could not control his sexual urges. We see only those people from the world we live in. But in the *Olam HaEmet*, the True World, Rabbi Akiva is always present. So even though we see Zimri in this portion, in this world, if we had the deeper vision of Moses, we would see only Rabbi Akiva. This reinforces the lesson we learned in the previous portion of Balak, that no matter what mistakes we have made in the past, the perfection of our souls is untouched.

According to a story in the *Talmud*, Rabbi Akiva had a sworn enemy, Turnus Rufus, Roman governor over all Judea. The bitter arguments between Turnus Rufus and Rabbi Akiva on such topics as circumcision, God's love for the Israelites and His hatred of idol worshipers, and the sacredness of Shabbat, were widely known, along with the fact that Rabbi Akiva always emerged the victor. Naturally, this only increased Turnus Rufus' hatred for Rabbi Akiva.

One day, Turnus Rufus came home very upset after one of his arguments with Rabbi Akiva, and his wife asked him what was wrong. He told her that he couldn't stand being bested by Rabbi Akiva anymore and that he wanted to destroy him. Turnus Rufus's wife said, "The Creator hates people who do negative sexual things. Certainly, if someone like Rabbi Akiva were to sleep with a married woman, this would be a terrible problem. If you give me permission, I will make sure Rabbi Akiva falls."

Her husband agreed, for his hatred of Rabbi Akiva was greater than any love he had for his wife. That evening, the wife of Turnus Rufus put on her most seductive finery and went to the home of Rabbi Akiva to seduce him. According to the *Talmud*, when Rabbi Akiva saw her, he did three things: He spat on the floor, he laughed, and he began to weep. Then he called on the soul of Elijah the Prophet to give him strength. The wife of Turnus Rufus asked Rabbi Akiva, "Why are you behaving this way?"

Rabbi Akiva replied, "I will explain to you why I did two of these things. I spat on the floor to remind me that we both come from insignificance, and I wept for the frailty of the human body, which decomposes in the earth." He did not explain to her the third thing—his laughter—but the *Talmud* tells us Rabbi Akiva laughed because, using the power of Divine Inspiration, he saw that after the death of Turnus Rufus, he and the governor's wife would eventually marry.

Through this conversation, Rabbi Akiva awakened something within the wife of Turnus Rufus, so she asked him if there was any way she could correct what she had just tried to do. When Rabbi Akiva said there was, she left to begin the process of correcting her ways. After Turnus Rufus died, she married Rabbi Akiva, and with the riches of the former governor, Rabbi Akiva was able to spread spiritual wisdom far and wide.

Rabbi Avraham Azulai explains that the wife of Turnus Rufus was the reincarnation of the soul of Kozbi, who had helped Zimri fall in a previous incarnation and who was also trying to make him fall in his incarnation as Rabbi Akiva. Were it not for his decision to call on the spiritual support of the soul of Elijah the Prophet, Rabbi Akiva might not have been able to withstand the sexual advances of the wife of Turnus Rufus. Why? Because Rabbi Akiva knew she was his soul mate, and the pull to be with her was therefore very strong. When she tried to seduce him, Rabbi Akiva was drawn to be with her, and only through the assistance of Pinchas/Elijah the Prophet was Rabbi Akiva able to restrict his desires. Because of this restriction, he not only merited the completion of his own correction, he merited the correction of his soul mate, the wife of Turnus Rufus (Kozbi), as well, which resulted in his being able to marry her.

These reincarnations and corrections of souls are part of a continuum connecting us with the source of all spiritual falling—the sin of Adam. The *Zohar* says at the time of Creation, Adam was supposed to have sexual relations with his wife, Eve, on the first Shabbat, but instead of waiting, he lay with her in the hours preceding Shabbat. If Adam and Eve had waited, perfection and not death would have been brought into the world.

The difference between perfection and death, between *bila hamavet lanetzach* and the pain and suffering that exists to this day, is the ability to restrict and say no. On the surface for Adam and Eve, everything looked correct: Eve was the soul mate of Adam, and they should be together. But they needed to restrict and wait until the appointed time to be together. The same is true of the wife of Turnus Rufus and Rabbi Akiva, but unlike Adam, Rabbi Akiva said no. And because of this restriction, he not only corrected his own soul, but he also completed the correction of his soul mate.

Rabbi Yonatan ben Uziel, who translated the Torah, with commentary, into Aramaic, tells us that the Creator made Pinchas into an angel who would live forever. Pinchas was chosen to be the one who would awaken the Final Redemption that foretells the coming of the *Gemar HaTikkun*. How did Pinchas merit this honor? Because Pinchas had the ability to feel the pain of the souls of others and was also willing to make any sacrifice to help correct those souls, the Creator said, "I have no choice but to keep you in this world until you correct them all." On the Shabbat of Pinchas, we can all receive from Pinchas this miraculous ability to correct our soul and to help with the correction of others.

It is inspiring to discover that the Shabbat of Pinchas is not simply the Shabbat of Pinchas, it is also the Shabbat of Rabbi Akiva. The *Midrash* says that when the Romans were in Israel, they forbade teaching the wisdom of the Torah and Kabbalah. But Rabbi Akiva continued to teach, and for this, he was arrested and put in jail. Every day, his student Rabbi Yehoshua haGarsi would go to the jail and attend to Rabbi Akiva's needs. On the eve of Yom Kippur, Rabbi Yehoshua had gone home to prepare when Elijah the Prophet came to him.

Elijah the Prophet informed Rabbi Yehoshua that his teacher, Rabbi Akiva, had left this world, and with that, Rabbi Yehoshua and Elijah the Prophet went to the jail. When they arrived, they witnessed a miracle: The doors to the jail were wide open, and the guards and other inmates were all asleep. Elijah and Rabbi Yehoshua went straight to Rabbi Akiva's cell, whereupon Elijah gently put the body of Rabbi Akiva over his shoulder and carried him out of the jail. Rabbi Yehoshua said to Elijah, "How can you put Rabbi Akiva on your shoulders? You are a priest, and no priest is allowed near a dead body."

Elijah the Prophet answered, "You should know, Rabbi Yehoshua, that no impurity comes to righteous souls or to their students." And so, with Rabbi Yehoshua by his side, Elijah carried the body of

Rabbi Akiva on his shoulders all night until the two men came to a cave in a mountain. When they got there, a miracle occurred. The cave opened, and inside they could see a room fully prepared for Rabbi Akiva, with a bed and chairs and a table with a candelabrum on it. Elijah the Prophet walked over to the bed and lovingly laid down the body of Rabbi Akiva. As he and Rabbi Yehoshua walked out, the candelabrum began to emanate a great Light, and the walls of the cave closed up behind them.

There are many righteous people whom Elijah the Prophet buried once they passed away, so why did he not just bury Rabbi Akiva? Why did he have to carry him through the night on his shoulders? Because Elijah knew that after thousands of years, the great soul of Rabbi Akiva had completed its correction, so Elijah went to find Rabbi Akiva's soul a suitable final resting place.

On this Shabbat, we can draw Light from the soul of Pinchas, which is the soul of Elijah the Prophet—a soul so full of love, a soul so willing to sacrifice to help other souls with their correction, that the Creator asked Pinchas to remain in this world forever.

MATOT-MASEI

With the exception of leap years in the kabbalistic calendar, the portion of Matot or "tribes" is read on the same Shabbat with the following portion of Masei or "journeys," which is why they are discussed together here. Matot-Masei are the last two chapters of the Book of Numbers, and they begin with a discussion of the laws regarding a vow or oath. At first, these chapters don't seem to address anything very important, but that in itself turns out to be the heart of a very significant matter. One clue we have about the weight of these portions is that they contain lessons that Moses taught in the last moments of his life. What could be so important that Moses would need to wait forty years to reveal it? What is so profound about the portions of Matot-Masei?

The key lesson that Moses gives us is that if we want to bind our soul to the Creator, we have to make sure that nothing in our life is mundane (as this portion appears to be), that everything is holy. When nothing in our life is mundane, including the negative thoughts that lead to negative actions, then everything we say, everything we pray for, and everything that comes out of our mouth will have the power of prophecy.

There are three primary aspects of our lives that we consider mundane: Thinking, eating, and basic activity. When we look at our thoughts, it's not easy to think of them as being holy—at least not all of them. What about our negative thoughts, which lead to negative actions? Don't they come from the darkness? If so, how could they possibly be holy?

In his commentary *Heichal HaBrachah*, Rabbi Yitzchak Isaac, the Komarno Rebbe, writes: "The most basic and most important understanding is that everything that happens in our life is from the Creator, and that every thought that comes into our mind is from the Creator." He goes on to explain further: "Even when a negative thought comes into our mind, urging us to take a negative action, we have to have certainty that the Light of the Creator is in this thought. Although this Light is covered by many layers of darkness, the essence of this thought is Light."

Often, when a negative thought comes to mind, we either fall spiritually by acting on it or we push the thought aside. But both these responses leave the thought uncorrected. How do we do that? Rabbi Yitzchak Isaac says, "When we think about the Light that lies within a dark thought, we transform it." When the thought comes and we stop long enough to realize it is the Light of the Creator covered by shells of darkness, we remove those shells, elevating the spark of Light within. But Rabbi Yitzchak Isaac also warns, "If we don't believe this and we don't do this, we remain in Egypt." If our job is to free the Light within negative thoughts, but we don't believe that negative thoughts are the Light of the Creator, then our minds are still in exile.

Rabbi Menachem Nachum of Chernobyl, the *Maor Einayim*, expands on this concept by observing that all of our spiritual work is "to make the territory of Holiness wider." He explains that to the degree that we do not see the Light of the Creator in everything, we diminish the domain of the Light of the Creator in this world. But as we come to see the Light of the Creator more and more, we expand the domain of holiness in our world. Therefore, it is vitally important that we see negative thoughts as Light.

Where do these sparks of Light in our negative thoughts come from? They are sparks we have thrown into the darkness when we acted on the Desire to Receive for the Self Alone, coming back in the form of negative thoughts so we can have this chance to correct them. Rabbi Yitzchak Isaac continues, "These sparks come to us so that we can elevate them to their source. When we just push the thought aside and don't do the work of transforming it and taking out the Light inside it, it is as if we are killing that spark of Light; we are taking that spark of Light that is standing right in front of us, begging us, 'Please, correct me,' and we are saying 'No. Go back into the darkness.'"

The second level of elevating sparks of Light is through our food. The *Maor Einayim* says that we must come to see the Light of the Creator in our food, difficult as that may be. He says that it is easy for us to acknowledge that prayer is holy because when we pray, our entire mind is focused on something spiritual. But eating is such a mundane activity that it's difficult to imagine a way to make it holy. What are we supposed to do—meditate or pray while we eat?

The *Maor Einayim* says that although some kabbalists do just that, all we need to do is acknowledge that we want to elevate the sparks of Light within the food we eat, just as we did with our thoughts.

This consciousness is our goal, and it extends to all types of food. We don't need to change anything about the way we eat. All we need to do is awaken the consciousness that while we are eating, we want to elevate the sparks of Light in our food so that when we undertake an act of selfless sharing, an act of revealing Light, these sparks of Light can also take part.

When the *Maor Einayim* says, "We have to know with absolute certainty that there is nothing that is not spiritual work," he could easily be talking about the third aspect of the mundane: Basic activity. Now that we know the level of consciousness we're aspiring to, we could be doing something as simple as watching a movie, knowing that the enjoyment we experience are the sparks of Light in the movie that we want to elevate. Studying the *Zohar* is without doubt a spiritually uplifting activity, but the lesson of Matot/Masei is not to change the way we conduct our lives so that we're reading the *Zohar* all the time, for example; the lesson here is to awaken the consciousness that there is nothing about our lives that is not holy.

When the tribes of Reuben, Gad, and the half-tribe of Manasseh got their portion of land across the Jordan River, on a deeper level, this last portion of the Book of Numbers is referring to the importance of extending the borders of Holiness. We do this by perfecting the consciousness that everything is holy, including watching a movie and reading magazines. There are certainly things in our life that aren't perfect, but they still lie within the Realm of Holiness. Everything isn't meant to be perfect, but everything is meant to be holy. Everything.

The *Maor Einayim* explains that when we see a person or situation as negative, we diminish the *gevul haKedushah*, the borders of Holiness in this world. We have to realize how powerful our consciousness is. How we see people and situations is crucial to whether we are going to expand the borders of Light or shrink them. When we revealed the Light within Korach and Bilaam in the previous portions, for example, we expanded the borders of Holiness. Our work is to keep expanding these borders, even in the most mundane aspects of daily life, including our thoughts, our food, and our daily activities. Our work is to keep expanding *gevul haKedushah*, the borders of Holiness, until we reach the *Gemar HaTikkun*.

DEUTERONOMY

DEVARIM

The kabbalists explain that there are three weeks of the year when the Light of the Creator is hidden, which run from the 17th of *Tammuz* (Cancer) until the 9th of *Av* (Leo). The 9th of *Av*, also known as *Tisha B'Av*, is the day both Temples in Jerusalem were destroyed and is regarded as the most negative day of the year.

Rabbi Avraham Yehoshua Heshil, the Apta Rebbe, says that the Shabbat of Devarim (also known as Shabbat *Chazon* or the "Shabbat of Vision") is the greatest Shabbat of the year. As support, he quotes a *Midrash* as saying: "There was no greater day for the Israelites than the day that the Temple was destroyed." How can a *Midrash* possibly make this claim? In addition to the psychic and spiritual damage, thousands of people were killed when the Temple was destroyed. The Apta Rebbe goes on to discuss a law in the *Talmud* that says that if a husband is going away on a long trip, he has to lie with his wife the night before he leaves. What does this have to do with the destruction of the Temples? The Apta Rebbe explains that whenever there is a separation, there also has to be an equally great union. Although *Tisha B'Av* was a tragic day in the physical world, it was a day of amazing unification in the Upper Worlds.

Rabbi Jacob Isaac Horowitz, the Chozeh of Lublin, confirms that wherever there is the greatest amount of darkness, there is also the greatest amount of Light. This is the case on *Tisha B'Av*, but on this day, the negativity blocks out the Light. The Shabbat before *Tisha B'Av* allows us to connect to just the positive aspect of *Tisha B'Av*—the greatest revelation of the Light of the Creator; this means that this great Light is revealed completely only on the Shabbat of Devarim.

The Book of Kings says: "And the Lord said to him [Elijah the Prophet], 'Go, return on your way to the wilderness of Damascus: and when you come, anoint Hazael to be king over Syria: And Jehu the son of Nimshi shall you anoint to be king over Israel: and Elisha the son of Shaphat of Abelmeholah shall you anoint to be prophet in your stead.' … So he departed there, and found Elisha the son of Shafat, who was plowing with twelve yoke of oxen before him, and he with the twelfth: and Elijah passed by him, and cast his mantle on him."

Although Elijah the Prophet never died, but simply left this physical plane, he had been commanded by the Creator to choose Elisha, the son of Shafat, to succeed him as the next prophet of the Israelites. Later, Elijah told Elisha that the Creator had told him it was time for him to leave this physical world; Elijah would no longer be the prophet and leader of that generation, and Elisha, the son of Shafat, would replace him. When that time approached, Elijah asked Elisha what he could do for him before he passed over. Elisha answered that he wanted a double portion of Elijah's spirit, to which Elijah replied,

"You have asked a hard thing: Nevertheless, if you see me when I am taken from you, it shall be so to you; but if not, it shall not be so." And it came to pass, as they still went on, and talked, that, behold, there appeared a chariot of fire, and horses of fire, and parted them both asunder; and Elijah went up by a whirlwind into Heaven. And Elisha saw it, and he cried, father, my father, the chariot of Israel, and the horsemen thereof. And he saw him no more."

In the *Zohar*, Rav Elazar says we need to pay special attention to this puzzling section. Elijah the Prophet asked Elisha what he wanted from him before he left this world, but it was not Elijah's role to give blessings to Elisha. Why did Elijah talk as if it were up to him whether Elisha would get blessings or not? This was the Creator's decision. And why did Elisha ask Elijah to give him double his strength? How can someone give something he doesn't have? The *Zohar* says that the first question is not really a question at all because Elijah knew that the Creator would do anything he asked. If Elijah wanted a blessing to come down, he could promise it and it would come.

Rav Ashlag provides an answer to the question of why Elisha asked Elijah for double his strength. Elisha *was* asking for something that lay within Elijah the Prophet's power, but it was a use of his strength that Elijah had never exercised before. Rav Ashlag says that in order to understand this, we have to delve into the *Zohar*. One of its most basic understandings is that it is the spiritual work of humanity to elevate the sparks of Light that fell at the time of the shattering of the Vessels after the sin of Adam. The kabbalists say that 320 sparks of Light fell at that time, and that when humanity finishes elevating these 320 fallen sparks, this will bring about the *Gemar HaTikkun* (the Final Correction). However, humankind can elevate only 288 of the 320 sparks that have fallen; we are not capable of elevating the remaining 32. These are still encased in their *klipot*, or negative shells, and it is not our job to free them.

Rav Ashlag explains that it is these last 32 sparks that keep death in this world. As things now stand, even when a person has finished his or her own personal *tikkun*, or correction, that person still has to die. Only a few special people—Elijah the Prophet being one—are able to correct their personal share of the last 32 fallen sparks. So how will the last 32 sparks be corrected? Astonishingly, Rav Ashlag says we won't need to do a thing. When we finish correcting the first 288 sparks of Light, the last 32 sparks of Light will correct on their own.

Rav Ashlag explains that every righteous person has a specific task, and when this task is completed, he or she leaves this world. He says that Elijah the Prophet is the channel for the correction of the 288 sparks that will trigger the rest. Therefore, what Elisha was asking for when he requested to have twice Elijah's strength was not only to be given the strength to reveal the global 288 fallen sparks, but to manifest the correction of the last 32 sparks as well. Rav Ashlag reveals that although at that time it was not the job of Elijah to correct the last 32 fallen sparks, because he had the power to correct the final 288th spark, he also had indirect control over the last 32 sparks, so Elisha's request was not unreasonable.

This story has many ramifications for our lives. One of them is the understanding that our greatest opportunity to reveal the *Gemar HaTikkun* will come at the most difficult time in our lives. We will have a chance to reach the remaining 32 fallen sparks only during the moment of greatest separation, when the greatest darkness is revealed in our lives. If we are able to maintain consciousness at this most difficult time, we will succeed.

One of the great gifts of this Shabbat of Devarim is that all of our spiritual strength can be doubled. One week before the 9th of Av, on the Shabbat that connects us to the greatest separation—the destruction of the Temples—we gain access to the most incredible Light. On this Shabbat, we have the power to double the strength of Elijah the Prophet.

VA'ETCHANAN

This portion of Va'etchanan, which means "and I besought," begins with Moses begging the Creator to let him enter into the land of Israel. "And I pleaded with the Creator at that time, saying, 'Creator, God, You have begun to show Your servant Your greatness, and Your strong hand; for what god is there in Heaven or on Earth, that can do according to Your works, and according to Your mighty acts? Let me go over, I pray You, and see the good land that is beyond the Jordan, those pleasant mountains and Lebanon."

We know that Moses originally intended to lead the Israelites not only out of Egypt and through the desert, but into the land of Israel as well. We also know that this never happened. According to the account given in the Torah, there came a moment in time when Miriam's well no longer followed the Israelites in the desert, so they had no water. The Creator told Moses to speak to a stone and a miracle would occur: Water would flow out for the Israelites to drink. As the story goes, instead of speaking to the stone, Moses hit it twice, but water still poured out.

In the Torah, the Creator tells Moses that because he did not perform the miracle as the Creator specified, he would not be allowed to lead his nation into the land of Israel. This is generally seen as a punishment, but the kabbalists have a different view. Rav Ashlag explains that the Israelites were not worthy of a more elevated miracle—of Moses speaking to the stone—because they were not yet on that spiritual level. So Moses had to hit the stone. Furthermore, not entering the land of Israel wasn't a punishment for Moses, but an indication that the Israelites were not elevated enough spiritually to merit Moses leading them into the land of Israel.

So why in this portion does Moses say, "I begged"? Moses certainly begs the Creator. He says, "Let me see the land. Let me enter and see the land." The Torah tells us that the Hebrew word used for Moses' prayer is *va'etchanan*, which has the numerical value of 515. The kabbalists say this means that Moses prayed 515 times to be allowed to see the new land of his people. Why was this so important to Moses, and why were his prayers not answered? The kabbalists explain that many times we pray for things, but our vision of what we need might not be accurate; we don't have the clarity to know how things should be. But the kabbalists also say that when a prayer comes from our soul, it is always answered. When we pray for things and don't receive them, it's because our soul did not join in our prayer.

When Moses prays, he says, "*Ve'er'eh et ha eretz hatova,*" or "Let me see the good land." We know that the Creator takes Moses to the top of a mountain, where He shows Moses all of the land, because this is what Moses' soul was asking for. So Moses' prayer was answered. On another level, the kabbalists explain that Moses was not asking to simply see *or* enter the land. This was not a physical land but a spiritual state, a state of perfection, and Moses knew that in order to enable the Israelites and all subsequent generations to awaken the Light of Israel, Moses needed to connect to it.

Therefore, when the text says that Moses was put on the mountain and he saw "the last ocean," *hayam ha'acharon*, those words actually mean *hayom ha'acharon*, or he saw "the last day." This confirms that Moses' vision of the land of Israel was not physical; instead, the Creator opened to him all the secrets, all the history, and all the elevations and fallings that lay ahead. The Creator showed Moses Jerusalem. The Creator showed him the First Temple. The Creator showed him the destruction of the First Temple. The Creator showed him the Second Temple, and the destruction of the Second Temple. The Creator showed him what is called the Third Temple, the Temple that will come down from the Heavens once humanity has achieved ultimate redemption. Thus Moses gained not only a vision of the future, but of the *Gemar HaTikkun*.

Why was this so important to Moses? Why did he pray 515 times to be given the opportunity to see the Promised Land? Here we learn another important lesson: That the only place where a person can correct, the only place where a person can elevate, is the physical world. In the Upper Worlds, there is no growth. An individual cannot do spiritual work to perfect the soul or to elevate it in the spiritual realms; that can only be accomplished in this world. Unfortunately, we think that we always have time: *I won't take this opportunity; I'll take one tomorrow.* We don't realize that we *don't* have limitless time to correct, to elevate, and to grow, for once our soul leaves this world, that opportunity is no more.

The Rav often uses the example of a vault filled with diamonds and gold, which opens up at regular times. Because this happens every single day, we don't ever feel any sense of urgency. It seems as if there will be an endless number of chances to haul away treasure, but there won't. Moses begs the Creator because he knows that this is the only place and now is the only time. We, on the other hand, take our opportunities for granted.

The other day, I was talking to one of our students about his parents, about how little time he spends with them. He had the best of reasons why he couldn't see them more often, and I shared with him that, according to the Torah, if a person honors and respects his or her parents, that person merits long life. And that's just the physical reward; the blessings and Light that a person can receive by sharing with his or her parents is limitless. I said to him, "You have a wide-open bank vault inviting you to take as much as you want, but it won't stay open forever."

The message of the portion of Va'etchanan is this: Seize your opportunities. They are not limitless, nor are they available everywhere. They can only be found here in this world. Whether it's our relationship with our parents, our children, or our friends, our chances to work on it are finite in number and infinitely precious. We need to beg for them.

EKEV

Usually the word *ekev* means "heel." In fact, this word shares the same three-letter root as the name of Jacob, who was born holding on to Esau's heel. However, in this third reading from the book of Deuteronomy, the word *ekev* means "on the heels of" or "because of." It is used in the first verse of the portion, which says: "And it shall come to pass, because you hearken to these ordinances and keep and do them, that the Creator, your God, shall keep with you the Covenant and the mercy which He swore to your fathers." This portion of Deuteronomy describes the good things that will happen for people on the heels of keeping to a spiritual path.

From a kabbalistic standpoint, this portion is about the power of unity and, specifically, the understanding that even the greatest souls cannot do on their own what far lesser souls can do if they have unity. Rabbi Kalonymus Kalman HaLevi Epstein, a student of the *Noam Elimelech*, says that in order for a group to be able to reveal great Light, it's important that no one individual views him- or herself as more important than anyone else. The smaller the ego, the greater the Light. He continues, "The person who views him- or herself as the ankles of the group is the one who is responsible for opening up the gates of blessings and the gates of abundance from Above."

This is true not only when we come together in spiritual matters; it is also true with family and in our work. The gift of this Shabbat is the understanding that nothing in the world can bring as much blessing as unity.

Rabbi Kalonymus Kalman Shapira of Piaseczno, the *Esh Kodesh*, says, "We know a person's desire draws Light from Above. When a person's desire is so strong it causes pain, that person can draw greater and more powerful Light." He goes on to say that, more importantly, the pain of this Holy desire breaks down any barriers we may have created through our Desire to Receive for the Self Alone. Rav Ashlag adds that the Hebrew word *ratzon*, or "desire," has the same letters as the word *tzinor*, the conduit or channel by which the Light of the Creator is revealed. On the Shabbat of Ekev, we have an opportunity to ask for the merit to truly own this teaching so that we can awaken a great desire and truly come to feel the pain of that desire; then we break down the barriers to the Light so it can come and manifest in our lives.

Rav Brandwein says the Bible uses the word *ekev*, or "heel," to indicate that our work is strictly about the diminishment of the self. What we want to awaken on this Shabbat is not just another understanding of how important it is to diminish our ego; we also want but to grasp the idea of being a heel, of being the lowest. As Rav Brandwein writes in a letter to the Rav: "I want to share with you something I shared on the week of Ekev, that having a diminished ego is the basis, the heel, of the entire spiritual structure.

Only someone who merits greater and greater diminishment of his ego merits hearing the words of the Creator."

Rav Brandwein taught the Rav that the greatest secrets are found in the places that are the least popular, the places that are the least comfortable. This lesson applies to finding a teacher as much as it does to our own spiritual work, but in both cases, one sure sign that our spiritual work is on the right track is its unpopularity. If our spiritual work is applauded by everyone, that's the time to question it. Rav Brandwein says that when we come down to this world, our soul is told to make sure that at least some of our spiritual work is unpopular.

On the Shabbat of Ekev, we see the power of unity, and we know that seeing ourselves as the weakest link in the chain allows us to be conduits for the Light of the Creator. We also become aware that feeling the pain of our soul—and of the souls of others—breaks down all the barriers our negative actions have erected between the Light of the Creator and ourselves. Most important of all is Rav Brandwein's revelation that all of our spiritual work is based on the diminishment of ego—on becoming the heel that supports the whole body.

RE'EH

The portion of Re'eh begins with: "Behold, I set before you this day a blessing and a curse." The sages teach us that since the time of the sin of Adam, everything in the world has become a mixture of good and evil, positive and negative. Today, everything we look at—every situation and every person—has both a good and a bad aspect. This means that at any given moment, we're given a choice to connect to the positive or the negative. What's more, whichever we choose to see—good or bad— is what we awaken within ourselves.

We need to understand that it is impossible for us to see something *outside* of ourselves that we do not first awaken *within* ourselves, for what we see reflects where we are in our consciousness. Moses was one of the greatest souls who ever lived, but if someone wanted to, he or she could find all kinds of negative things in Moses. And unfortunately, throughout all the time they spent in the desert, many Israelites did just that. But what were these Israelites actually seeing? They were awakening their own darkness, which was connecting to the shell of darkness around Moses, to the *klipot* that all of us have. There is a little good and a little bad in everything and everyone. The question is: Which one are we choosing to see?

Taking this idea a step further, it turns out that how we view the world and the people around us actually influences what happens next. If we choose to focus on the good in a person, for instance, we not only connect ourselves to the Light of the Creator, we also awaken positive energy in the other person. And, of course, when we only see the darkness in a person, we cause separation—in that person and in ourselves.

One of the best ways we can choose to support the positive aspect of life is through financial generosity. In the portion of Re'eh, the Bible says: "If there be among you a poor man, of one of your brothers, within any of your gates in your land which the Lord, your God gives you, you shall not harden your heart, nor shut your hand from your poor brother: But you shall open your hand wide to him, and shall surely lend him sufficient for his need, in that which he wants. ... You shall surely give him, and your heart shall not be grieved when you give to him: because for this thing the Lord, your God shall bless you in all your works, and in all that you put your hand to."

The *Talmud* says that the nature of the world is cyclical: The Light we reveal through an action of giving away money will come back to us in a positive way. In the Book of Prophets, we read that whenever King Saul went to seek Samuel the Prophet so that Samuel could pray for him, King Saul would always ask what he could give to Samuel. The *Talmud* reiterates this point: "If a person is having difficulties, he should go to a wise and righteous person and ask him to pray for him. But if a person does not first give something to the righteous person, the prayers of that righteous person cannot have an effect."

Rav Elazar explains that all the difficulties we experience in our lives fall into three categories: Family (children and relationships); life (health issues); and sustenance (money issues). The reason we lack Light in these areas is because we have somehow cut ourselves off from these blessings through our negative actions. So how do we correct this? Rav Elazar says we do it through prayer, and that the prayer of a righteous person is especially effective. But how can a righteous person restore someone else's broken connection? Rav Elazar says that the only way this can work is if the person in need somehow gives over some part of his or her essence to the righteous person. Although there are other ways to do this, Rav Elazar is talking here about the importance of charity. When someone gives a righteous person something that's important to him or her—and, for most people, this is money—the righteous person now has the ability to reconnect him or her to their source because now the righteous person has part of their essence.

On the Shabbat of Re'eh, we are reminded that we make a powerful choice every time we decide if a person or situation is bad or good. And when we put ourselves on the side of the good, we can further tip the balance by giving both our money and our prayers.

SHOFTIM

The portion of Shoftim begins with the words: "Judges and officers shall you make in all your gates...and they shall judge the nation with just judgment [*mishpat tzedek*]." The word *tzedek*, translated literally, means "just." But Rabbi Levi Yitzchak of Berditchev, the *Kedushat Levi*, says, "Unfortunately, there is a tremendous amount of judgment in our world. The ultimate purpose of our spiritual work is to diminish darkness and awaken more mercy in the world. And how do we accomplish this? When we act with mercy, when we judge others in a merciful way, we open up the Gates of Mercy Above to bring down blessings."

Although opening the Gates of Mercy is something we may have heard about before, it's important to understand just how vital this is for us, especially as we come into the month of *Elul* (Virgo), the month when judgments we have created through our previous negative actions can come down on us. The *Kedushat Levi* makes it clear to us that by proactively judging others in a positive way, we open up the Gates of Mercy for ourselves as well as for others. And the opposite holds true as well: Every time we judge someone negatively, we open up the Gates of Judgment and bring more darkness, pain, and death into the world. The judgment that exists in the world today is partly our responsibility.

The month of *Elul* is the time when we do our own internal work to remove judgment from our lives before *Rosh Hashanah.* It is no coincidence that the portion of Shoftim is always read in the month of *Elul.* Awakening this new consciousness in *Elul* protects us from all the judgments that might be there for us because of our prior negative actions.

When it comes to choosing to see the positive, we find a wonderful example in the Book of Proverbs, when King Solomon says, "Go look at the ant, and through her ways, you will become wise." The *Midrash* provides some interesting facts about ants. An ant lives for only six months, and during this time, eats only one and a half grains of wheat. Yet the ant spends most of its life gathering a vast supply of wheat and barley. Why? The reason the ant gathers more food than it could ever eat in its lifetime is because it knows that one day, people are going to usher in immortality, and when that day comes, the ant wants to be sure to have enough food. King Solomon tells us that the ant has more certainty and knowledge of immortality than we do; otherwise, we would be conducting our lives in a completely different way.

Awakening the immortality consciousness of the ant is one of the gifts of the Shabbat of Shoftim. Making that choice—or any other choice, whether positive or negative— affects what comes next in our lives. So, too, does the power of certainty.

KI TETZE

In the portion of Ki Tetze, the Creator reveals to us how we can aspire to the level of *umateh elokim beyadi*, where we have the power to ward off judgments like pain, sickness, and even death. Most of us are not at this level yet, but we can begin by asking ourselves if we believe that this level is even possible. Rabbi Naftali of Ropshitz asks, "What is the spiritual logic behind this ability to cast aside judgment? And how do we actually do it?" In order to answer this question, we have to go back to the fact that each of us has two aspects, two forms of energy. The *Zohar* says that each Name of the Creator is a channel for different forms of Light. The Name *Yud, Hei, Vav,* and *Hei* (the Tetragrammaton) is a channel for mercy: In Kabbalah, this is known as Right Column energy. The Name *Elohim* indicates judgment, which is Left Column energy. To put it more directly, the Desire to Share—the Light of the Creator—is Right Column energy. The Desire to Receive for the Self Alone is Left Column energy.

Rabbi Naftali says that the purpose of Creation was to give us the free will to engage in a battle between the Right Column (the Desire to Share) and the Left Column (the Desire to Receive). When we act the "right way," we push down our natural Desire to Receive for the Self Alone by increasing the power of the Right Column over the Left. So when we say that there is a "right way" to do something, on a deeper level we're pointing out the potential to elevate the Right Column over the Left Column. In any given situation, we have two choices: We can allow the Left Column to rule over the Right, or we can say, "No. I'm going to subdue my ego; I'm going to raise up my Desire to Share." And we have hundreds of opportunities each day to decide whether we are going to go Right or Left.

What happens if we're successful in continually pushing down the Left Column in favor of the Right? Since we know that each person is a mirror for the entire world, strengthening the Right Column in our lives can give us the power to cast off judgments, not just our own but those that would otherwise come to those around us. When we choose Right over Left Column, so too do we receive the power to open up the Light of the Right Column, to overwhelm the judgments of the Left Column. How we act in our individual lives is a reflection of our agency in the world and vice versa.

Imagine that today we have five opportunities to choose to go with either the Left Column or the Right. A friend calls us at work very upset; we're busy, but we know that our friend is struggling and we can help. Our ailing mother wants us to come visit on a weekend when we've already made plans with friends. We get a call from the local blood bank that they're running short of our rare blood type. Our spouse has left some important papers on his desk at home and we're much closer to the house than he is; can we make the trip to pick them up? A potential client has heard about us through a mutual friend and would like to meet right away, but she is not in a position to pay our usual fee. If we choose Right over Left in most, if not all, of these occasions, we are earning the ability to limit judgments in this world. Our Desire to Share is mirrored back in the form of mercy, whereas our Desire to Receive is mirrored back as more judgments for ourselves and for the world.

If in our personal life, we are mostly successful in our battle to have the Right Column prevail over the Left, we are then given the power of *umateh elokim beyadi*, the power to ward off judgments for ourselves and for others. Then we can even see someone who is sick or in pain and push these judgments away, bringing blessings instead. The Light of *umateh elokim beyadi* is the gift revealed to us on the Shabbat of Ki Tetze. With this Light, we can set judgment aside, as Rav Shimon bar Yochai did with the Angel of Death when he saw him dancing in front of Rabbi Yitzchak. Rav Shimon pushed the Angel of Death—the ultimate expression of the Left Column—out of the house so he could not harm Rabbi Yitzchak. Although we are not yet at the level of Rav Shimon bar Yochai, nonetheless all spiritual development begins with understanding. In this case, we can see the benefit of choosing the Right Column over the Left, and we recognize the spiritual logic of the mirror and how it can help support and implement this new power.

Rabbi Naftali tells us that when the portion of Ki Tetze says, "When you go out to battle against your enemy, and the Creator, your God, delivers them into your hands...," it is not referring to an external enemy. It's addressing the benefit of fighting our own Desire to Receive for the Self Alone, our own Left Column. It is through this struggle and our awareness of why we are engaged in it that the Creator will give each of us the power to push aside judgments. The Creator will deliver our enemy into our hands.

There are lots of people who are on a spiritual path, who work constantly to give the Right Column dominance over the Left. But what about those other people whom the *Zohar* calls *Neshamot ha'ashukot*, those souls that are deeply enmeshed in the negative side, who are under the control of the Left Column? The Bible verse continues with *veshavita shivyo*, "and you carry them away captives," meaning that once we have the power of *umateh elokim beyadi*, we also have the power to rescue even those souls that are deeply under the control of the judgment of the Left Column. Usually there is only so much we can give to others in terms of either helping them understand or giving them tools to do their own spiritual work. But in the portion of Ki Tetze, we learn how to free souls that are not ready to do it on their own.

It helps us do battle with the Left Column when we remember that everything and everyone—good and bad—contains a spark of the Light of the Creator. In a person or situation ruled by the Left Column, the spark of Light has become surrounded by negativity, like a small balloon that expands as we blow air into it. When we take a little pin to it, however—something we can often do through simple awareness—this huge balloon becomes insignificant. This tells us that negativity is mostly an illusion; there is almost nothing there. When we can rescue the tiny spark of the Light of the Creator inside a problem, the problem itself disappears, no matter how huge it might have seemed.

Our consciousness and level of clarity determine whether something is a big problem or no problem at all. A number of sages famously believe that when the *Gemar HaTikkun* (the Final Correction) comes, there will be no huge shift in consciousness. A tiny shift will be enough to reveal to us that there was no problem to begin with. These same sages say that when the Resurrection of the Dead takes place, we are going to realize how silly we were to have ever thought that all those people who left the world were actually gone. So if we think that the battle to change this world and to bring the *Gemar HaTikkun* pits us against a vast and powerful army of negativity, we're in for a long, tough fight. But if we think that there is almost nothing between us and the *Gemar HaTikkun*, and that all the problems we see are just tiny sparks of Light inflated to look like big obstacles, then that's what we'll be facing.

There are three stages in any conflict: We prepare for battle; we fight the battle; and then we win or lose the battle. So why does the portion of Ki Tetze mention only two stages: The beginning and the end? What happened to the actual fighting? The Bible says: "If you go out to battle, you have won the battle." What this means is that if we're willing to face our enemy, we'll find that our enemy doesn't really exist. When we truly understand that despite appearances, there is no challenge—there is only a tiny spark of Light trapped in a puffed-up illusion—we will have won.

On the Shabbat of Ki Tetze, we need to ask the Creator to give us the strength and clarity to see the difference between what is real and what is illusion. We also have to direct this consciousness inward; to identify what aspects of ourselves we want to cleanse. Whatever blessings we want to receive have to be awakened while we are still in the month of *Elul*, the month of *teshuvah*, of repentance, for *Rosh Hashanah* marks the first day of *Tishrei* and the cosmic time of judgment.

The sages explain that there is always a deep connection between discussions that are near each other in the Bible. In the portion of Ki Tetze, verses 25:14-16 explain that we have to be meticulously honest in our business dealings. Immediately following these verses, we find a section about the nation of Amalek. Rashi says that these two sets of verses are telling us that if we have cheated, then we should worry about the power of Amalek bringing judgments into our life. But we can ward off those judgments in the month of *Elul* if we strengthen the Right Column, if we see beyond appearances, and we do not lie to ourselves.

So the month of *Elul* is about truth. If we are truthful about who we are and what we have done, then on *Rosh Hashanah* and *Yom Kippur*, only the things we have forgotten to consider will be judged. Therefore, in the month of *Elul*, we have to make sure that we remember everything because whatever we awaken, whatever we remember, whatever truth we look at directly, will not bring judgment into our lives.

The *Zohar* says that there is no other time of the year when the Creator is as close to us. Rashi explains that the Creator joins us in *teshuvah* during the month of *Elul* because even the Creator sometimes feels bad about the fact that he created the evil inclination, the Desire to Receive for the Self Alone.

There is a famous parable in the *Zohar* about a king who wanted to test his son's faith to help him grow spiritually. The king asked a prostitute to tempt his son, but unfortunately, the son succumbed to her advances, failing the test. Upon hearing what had happened, the king felt badly that he had brought this pain to his son. The only reason the king had arranged this scenario was to help his son elevate, but his son fell instead, and now both he and the king were suffering.

When the Creator sees that we are being truly honest with ourselves in the month of *Elul*, that we are doing the work of this month, that we repent and feel sorry for our selfish actions of the past year, the Creator says, "I, too, feel bad for the pain that I have caused My children." When we awaken pain for what we have done, the Creator awakens pain for putting us in this situation, and that pain of the Creator removes all the sparks of Light that we have put in the negative side. Then He gives them back to us. This is the awesome power of *teshuvah* in the month of *Elul.*

KI TAVO

In Deuteronomy, we read: "And Moses charged the people the same day, saying: 'These shall stand upon Mount Gerizim to bless the people, when you have crossed over the Jordan: Simeon and Levi, and Judah and Issachar, and Joseph and Benjamin; and these shall stand upon Mount Ebal for the curse: Reuben, Gad, and Asher, and Zebulun, Dan, and Naftali." The *Zohar* explains that the curses being referred to here do not mean the Creator is going to punish someone, but rather that if a person does something that awakens darkness, that darkness will manifest in his or her life.

To help us understand this point, we turn to Rav Isaac Luria, the Ari. In his volume *Gates of Meditation*, the Ari speaks about the Light revealed in different prayers. He explains that a tremendous amount of Light shines forth from the Torah when we lift it up and look at it prior to reading it. One of the obstacles we set in our own way is the fact that we don't have enough appreciation for the power of the spiritual tools we have been given. The reason why it seems strange to include not lifting up the Torah on the list of major transgressions is that we aren't tuned in to the tremendous amount of Light revealed every Shabbat when we lift up the Torah. If we were able to see it, the importance of this oversight would be easier to understand.

One of the lessons we want to take from this portion is a greater appreciation for actions that seem small but reveal tremendous amounts of Light. Not so many years ago, almost no one was aware of the spiritual tool of scanning the *Zohar*. The Rav received a message from the Upper Worlds that he should let people know that simply looking over the words of the *Zohar*—without reading or understanding them—brings a tremendous amount of Light. This seemingly minor action has made an enormous difference in the world.

The portion of Ki Tavo says: "And it shall be, when you enter into the land which the Creator, your God, gives you for an inheritance, and do possess it, and dwell therein; that you shall take of the first of all the fruit of the ground, which you shall bring in from your land that the Creator, your God, gives you; and you shall put it in a basket and shall go unto the place which the Creator, your God, shall choose to cause His name to dwell there. And you shall come to the priest that shall be in those days, and say to him: 'I profess this day unto the Creator, your God, for I have come to the land that God has sworn to our forefathers to give us.' And the priest shall take the basket out of your hand, and set it down before the altar of the Creator, your God." This passage means that anyone who owned a field and began growing produce would have to take the best examples of their first crop and travel to Jerusalem to bring these first fruits (*bikurim*) to the priest (*Kohen*).

In ancient times, such a journey could easily take days or weeks. The kabbalists make it clear that the owner of the field could not choose to send someone else in his stead; he had to make this journey himself. What is the reason for this different process? In the *Midrash*, Rashi tells us that the reason for the farmer bringing the *bikurim*, the first fruits, from wherever he may be living all the way to Jerusalem is simple: To show that he is grateful for the blessings he has been given. Most of us know that appreciation is generally a good thing, and we may even know that when a person is ungrateful, he pushes down all the blessings that are waiting to come into his life. But we may not be aware that when we express gratitude through action, rather than just through words, we generate a great deal of Light. This is one more case of something seemingly minor having a huge impact.

In the portion of Ki Tavo, Moses tells the Israelites, in effect, "You have a field, you have a family, you have blessings, so don't just wake up in the morning and thank the Creator; that's not enough. Do something to express your appreciation in a tangible way. Travel to Jerusalem with the finest of your first fruits and vegetables. Taking action based on gratitude will assist you in your transformation and lead to more blessings."

The *Midrash* says that after Jacob was saved from both his father-in-law and from the murderous rage of his brother, Esau, he left the city of Sukkot and opened up a shop where he sold high-quality merchandise at very low prices. The *Midrash* asks why Jacob, one of the spiritual giants of history, chose to open a shop. He did so to express his appreciation for the blessings that the Creator had given him. He knew that he could do some good by making expensive goods available to those who couldn't ordinarily afford them.

After Rav Shimon bar Yochai, the author of the *Zohar*, came out of the cave where he and his son had been hiding from the Romans for thirteen years, he went to the city of Tiberius, which in those days was considered spiritually impure. There he set about finding ways to rid the city of its negative ways. He then went on to many different cities on the same mission, making daily life for many people much easier. Why would Rav Shimon bar Yochai, the author of the *Zohar*, who had just revealed the most powerful Light in the history of humanity, take on the job of spiritual sanitation engineer? Because he was so overwhelmed by the blessings in his life that he had to do something active to express his appreciation.

The Shabbat of Ki Tavo teaches us to find ways to make the most of the spiritual tools available to us. We know that the Torah contains great Light. How can we do more with it? The Rav found a way when he encouraged people to use the *Zohar* by scanning it. Even a simple spiritual tool like appreciation can reveal new Light if we don't settle for expressing it in words, but take action to show our gratitude.

It's not easy to find new ways to use old tools, but one good way to approach this challenge is with what Buddhists call "Beginner's Mind." In the portion of Ki Tavo, Moses speaks to the Israelites a few days before he is about to leave this world and says, "*Hayom hazeh* ("This day"), the Creator is giving you all the spiritual work, all the spiritual tools, all the spiritual lessons." Now the Israelites had been given many lessons prior to this day and would be given many more after it, so what did Moses mean here? Moses is telling the Israelites—and us—that if we want to be able to connect to the Light of the Creator, then every spiritual act we undertake, every lesson we learn, every prayer we utter, has to be viewed as if today we are doing it for the first time. We need to make it brand new.

Everything in this world contains an inner aspect—a spark of the Light of the Creator—as well as an external aspect known as the *klipa*, or shell. The kabbalists teach us that new Light is infused in everything in this world every single day. Most people are much more excited on the first day of their marriage than they are on their thirtieth wedding anniversary, but in that thirtieth year, the Creator is sending in new Light the same as ever; if that couple connected to it, they could be even more excited than they were on their wedding night. Each time we read from the Torah, the Creator injects new Light into the reading, and if we accessed this Light, we could be more excited by the Torah today than ever before.

This is also true of the *Zohar*. Every time we open it up, the Creator imbues it with new Light, and by tasting this Light we get more and more excited about the *Zohar*. The reason we have to make an effort to awaken Beginner's Mind is that all too often, we fall into a rut, which means we are attaching ourselves to the shell and not to the Light. This Light is being made new every day—in our jobs, in our spiritual work, in our love relationships. Once we get past the shell, the *klipa*, our connection to the Light becomes more exciting every day. Rabbi Elimelech of Lizhensk, the great kabbalist also known as *Noam Elimelech*, says that every morning before we wake up, the Creator creates a package of new blessings, of new Light, of new mercies, of new kindness, and new goodness for each of us. But Rabbi Elimelech asks, "How do we merit receiving those blessings, that Light? We have to be *like* this new Light."

We have to be "like new" to receive the blessings that have been prepared for us today. It's just that simple. Start every day by taking a moment to ground yourself in the here-and-now. When you do, you will realize that you have never been in this moment before; it's unique, so savor every aspect of its newness. If you open up the

Zohar, take a moment to realize what's really going on: *I'm not reading Zohar today like I read it yesterday, or the day before, or a week ago. As I open up the Zohar, I know that the Creator is injecting new Light into these words. And that the Light that I'm going to experience is something I've never experienced before, that has never been in this world before.* This is the consciousness that connects us to new Light. And it is true, not just about the *Zohar* but about everything in our lives.

On the Shabbat of Ki Tavo, we want to tap into the consciousness of newness. As Moses is about to leave this world, he sums up all the wisdom he has been teaching for forty years by saying, "Live every moment of every day as if it were new." On this Shabbat, the Creator is asking us to use all the spiritual tools as if they were new, too. And by living fully in this moment, we can experience a taste of immortality.

NITZAVIM

In some years, Nitzavim, the fifty-first reading from the Torah, is read together with the next portion, Vayelech. As we saw in the portion of Ki Tetze, one of the most important supporting structures for our spiritual work is *teshuvah*, or repentance. Most of us think that the process of *teshuvah* is just about what we need to change, what we need to do differently. Although this is very important, Rabbi Kalonymus Kalman HaLevi Epstein, the *Maor Vashemesh*, a student of Rabbi Elimelech of Lizhensk, tells us that changing how we view others is even more important. If we are focused only on ourselves, it is not *teshuvah*.

Hopefully, we have all undergone the process of *teshuvah* for our negative actions this year, but if we are honest with ourselves, we know we're not going to be able to cleanse ourselves of *all* our negative deeds. If we still have baggage from this year, then the abundance and blessings that are meant to come to us on *Rosh*

Hashanah may not be able to make it past the negative angels we have created. So what can we do?

Rav Brandwein taught my father, the Rav, the concept of *HaShem tzilchah*, "the Light of the Creator is our shadow," which says that the way the Creator acts with us is dependent on how we act with other people. *HaShem tzilchah* means that how we look at, judge, and interact with other people is exactly how the Creator will look at us on *Rosh Hashanah*. The *slichot* prayers that we recite every day in the month of *Elul* say that one of the qualities of the Creator is *ve'over al peshah*, which literally means that the Creator skips over anything negative that we have done. How can this possibly be the case? This sounds like a violation of the Universal Law of cause and effect that is the very basis of Kabbalah: If a person acts in a negative, selfish way, he or she creates negative angels, which then show up in the person's life. So how can the Creator skip over our negative actions, letting them go by as if they don't exist? The answer lies in the fact that on *Rosh Hashanah*, the Creator doesn't judge us, but instead He looks at our lives to see if we have created a reality of *ve'over al peshah*. If we're skipping over the negativity of others, the Creator will return the favor.

A lot of the negativity we're working through in our own lives today may have more to do with past lifetimes than with anything we may be doing now, a theme that is nicely illustrated in a famous story about the Baal Shem Tov.

One of the students of the Baal Shem Tov came to his teacher and said, "I'm at my wit's end. I have so many problems in my life. I'm always short of money. I'm constantly fighting with my wife. I don't even enjoy my children. What can I do?"

So the Baal Shem Tov told him to go to a distant town and look for a certain person who could surely help him. The student was delighted. He knew that the Baal Shem Tov could make miracles, so he left town confident that his problems were on their way to being solved.

The student traveled for three days until he reached the village named by the Baal Shem Tov. There he began asking if anyone knew the person he was looking for. But to his surprise, no one had ever heard of this person. Finally, someone told the student of a very old man who had been living in the town since he was born; perhaps this man could help.

So the student went to the old man's home and asked him if he had ever heard of the person he was looking for. The moment he mentioned the name, the old man glared at him and spat on the ground. His face reddened and he said, "I don't ever want to hear that person's name mentioned in this house again. May all traces of his existence be wiped from the earth forever." The student was shocked and asked the old man what this person could possibly have done. The old man explained that this man had lived in the town approximately seventy years before and that he was the worst person imaginable. He was a thief. He was a liar. He was a cheat.

Confused, upset, and disappointed, the student set off on the long journey home. When he finally arrived in Mezibuz, he rushed to the Baal Shem Tov's home and knocked on the door. When he was ushered into the Baal Shem Tov's study, he told his teacher the whole story. The Baal Shem Tov then turned to his student and said, "I want you to know that this negative person was you in your last incarnation. All this trouble you are experiencing in this lifetime has nothing to do with your actions now and everything to do with what you did then."

The student of the Baal Shem Tov had to travel a great distance to find his past, but you and I have easier ways of finding ours. All we have to do is look at the most annoying people in our life today. In them, we see our *tikkun* reflected back to us: The work we need to do in order to correct from our last lifetime—or the one before that. Rav Moshe Chaim Ephraim Rav of Sudilkov, grandson of the Baal Shem Tov, writes: "My grandfather told me that most of us know that we are not new souls. We are old souls who have lived in this world many times. Therefore, whether we are aware of it or not, we all carry baggage today from those previous incarnations."

So how do we get rid of this baggage? The first step, as always, is to recognize it for what it is. We know there are no coincidences, so why do people with the same kinds of negative qualities keep showing up in our lives? If someone close to us treats people with less than human dignity, for example, the Creator is bringing this person to us for a reason. We may not be behaving that way now, but it's very likely that in our previous incarnation, or in the one before that, we behaved this way ourselves.

Cleaning up old negativity is a three-step process. First, don't judge other people. As we know, passing judgment blocks Light. Having the consciousness of *ve'over al peshah* helps keep our baggage from the past from wreaking havoc with our life today. Secondly, when we see someone doing something negative, we should try to help that person. Last, if we cannot help the other person, we should pray for him or her.

Although it is important not to judge others, it is just as important to understand why. The message of the Shabbat of Nitzavim is that there are many reasons for this, including cleansing ourselves of the selfish acts we committed in past incarnations. But the most important reason of all, as we approach *Rosh Hashanah,* is our awareness that as we act, so acts the Creator.

VAYELECH

In the portion of Vayelech, we hear sorrow in the voice of Moses: "For when I shall bring them into the land which I swore to their fathers, flowing with milk and honey; and they shall have eaten their fill and waxen fat; and turned to other gods and served them, and despised Me and broken My Covenant; then it shall come to pass, when many evils and troubles have come upon them that this song shall testify before them as witness; for it shall not be forgotten out of the mouths of their offspring; for I know the inclination of their behavior even now before I have brought them into the land which I swore to give them."

We see much the same dark sentiment in the *Talmud* when all the remaining sages got together in Kerem BeYavneh after the destruction of the Temple in Jerusalem and the Roman massacre. They were not just worried that the Torah would be forgotten; they thought this might be the end of the spiritual path for humanity. But the strong voice of Rav Shimon bar Yochai shored them up, saying, "No! You are wrong. There is no chance that the Torah and this wisdom will be neglected. The proof is in the pages of the Torah itself, in the words of the portion of Vayelech: *ky lo tishakach mipi zaro*, "the true path will never be forgotten."

The beleaguered sages probably knew that the physical Torah and the *Zohar* would continue to exist. What concerned them was the future. With darkness all around them, they couldn't see how real change—achieving the level of *devekut*—was going to take place. But when Rav Shimon bar Yochai stood before them and said, "*K**y** l**o** tishaka**ch** mip**i** zar**o***," he awakened this consciousness in the world. When we read this verse literally, it doesn't make much sense: "For it shall not be forgotten out of the mouths of their offspring." Whose offspring is the Torah talking about? But then we see that the last letters of these words spell the word *yochai*. The Torah is speaking about the offspring of Rav Shimon bar Yochai himself.

In the portion of Vayelech we see that Moses himself held out little hope for the Israelites, much the way the sages after the destruction of the Temple despaired of the spiritual future of humankind. But in the face of all this darkness, Rav Shimon bar Yochai revealed the *Zohar*. He himself stood up against doubt and fear, reminding those who remained that their truth would not be forgotten.

As we consider the Shabbat of Vayelech, we see that one of its great lessons is to appreciate the gift of the soul of Rav Shimon bar Yochai. The Shabbat of Vayelech reminds us that when we connect to the *Zohar*, we are not just scanning or reading it as part of our spiritual work, but that this legacy of Rav Shimon bar Yochai is the shining hope of humanity. If we are deepening our connection to the soul and promise of Rav Shimon bar Yochai—*ky lo tishakach mipi zaro*—then all the spiritual work we do will not be forgotten, nor will it fall on deaf ears.

HA'AZINU

The Shabbat of Ha'azinu falls between *Rosh Hashanah* and *Yom Kippur*. As we explore the spiritual significance of the portion of Ha'azinu, it's important to be aware of the process our souls are going through during this crucial ten-day period. Rav Isaac Luria, the Ari, explains that the key to understanding *Rosh Hashanah* lies in the story of Adam and Eve. When Adam and Eve are born back to back, God puts Adam to sleep in a state known as *dormita* so that He can literally cut Adam and Eve apart, separate them from one another. Kabbalistically, we see *Zeir Anpin*, or Supernal Man, being put to sleep spiritually, and then the judgments, or *dinim*, are cut away from *Zeir Anpin* and given to *Malchut*, the Supernal Female, who turns them into Light.

Cutting away the dark aspects of ourselves is part of what we go through during *Rosh Hashanah*. Then, in a second step that mirrors the process of *dormita*, we transform this darkness of judgment into Light. The *Zohar* states that *Rosh Hashanah* is the time when the Creator sits on the Throne of Judgment, and that from this day through to and including *Yom Kippur*, we have a unique opportunity and ability to transform our own awakened judgment into Light.

The Ari explains this process as follows. After we have become reborn by participating in the spiritual process of *Rosh Hashanah*, we cut away the lowest parts of ourselves. Now they can no longer attach themselves to judgment, to the results of our selfish actions throughout the year. Now that we have been through *Rosh Hashanah*, we don't have to go back to any of our negativity. We don't have to go back to any of our negative traits.

The kabbalists teach us that not only does our every negative action create a negative angel, but this angel remains with us for life. So what happens on *Rosh Hashanah*? Do we kill these negative angels? On *Rosh Hashanah*, we disconnect from these negative angels by elevating to a higher place. Here the negative angels we have created can no longer touch us—providing we don't go back to them. But they still exist in a lower realm, in the place we were before *Rosh Hashanah*. The gift of *ya'arof kamatar likchi*, which means "we will cut off," is to encourage us to stay clear of these negative angels by avoiding our former selfish behaviors. The way to make sure that we keep these dark forces from re-attaching to our lives is to see to it that our lives actually change.

There is a remarkable section of the *Zohar* that has a direct bearing on this aspect of the Shabbat of Ha'azinu that we've been exploring. It's known as "Locks, Entryways, and Beautiful Chambers."

There are times when we feel closed off from joy, as if the passageways to it are closed and locked. At other times, we feel we're making progress in our lives, as though we're taking advantage of an opening or an entryway. And finally, there are those incredible moments when we feel ecstatic, as if we had just found our way into the vast open chambers that the *Zohar* calls *heichalot*, full of happiness and Light. Most of us think of these three experiences as being separate from each another, but Rav Ashlag says this way of thinking about our lives is incorrect.

Locks are energy that we experience as separating us from the Light of the Creator. But a lock and an entryway are made of the same energy, and they're even found in the same location. All the locks that seem to be separating us from the Light of the Creator are actually openings. When we hit a difficult place or situation in life, we want to avoid it, but if we do, we've missed an entryway. What's more, we're only given so many locks and entryways in this lifetime, and if we keep avoiding them, we'll never enter the *Heichal*, the vast and beautiful Chamber of the Light of the Creator.

We didn't come into this world just to walk around locks and challenges. We are supposed to push ourselves when things get difficult. *And there is no opening unless we go through a lock.* As Rav Ashlag puts it, "Every doubt, every difficulty, every paradox that we work through, becomes an opening for wisdom, for Light, for blessings." And no lock is the same. Every lock is uniquely wrought to provide us with a special opening. When we sidestep today's challenge, we'll find a different one next week—but this week's opportunity will be lost.

The gift of the Shabbat of Ha'azinu is that we can turn the judgment that we removed on *Rosh Hashanah* into Light. We can see locks for what they are, and we can use them as entryways. Now each of these locks becomes a Gate of Righteousness, a gate through which we and the world can both pass because the gates we create aren't just for us. What we have opened up is a Chamber of Light for the world.

Rav Ashlag explains that there is a related concept called *teshuvah me'ahava,* when a person undertakes the process of spiritual correction out of love. As I was preparing for *Rosh Hashanah* this year and thinking about the Shabbat of Ha'azinu, I realized that there is another way to understand this love that leads to spiritual correction—not as a love of the Creator, but as a love of the darkness we have created. From the elevated place we are in today, we can look back at the negative actions of this year and realize that not only can we separate ourselves from the chaos that they might create, but we can also transform them. We can turn locks into entryways.

Changing darkness into Light, bitterness into sweetness: This is the power of the Shabbat of Ha'azinu.

VEZOT HABRACHA

In this week's portion of Vezot HaBracha, we have the last eight verses in the Torah: "So Moses, the servant of the Lord, died there in the land of Moab, according to the word of God. And he was buried in the valley in the land of Moab over against Beth-Peor; and no man knows of his grave to this day. And Moses was a hundred and twenty years old when he died: his eye was not dim, nor his natural force abated. And the children of Israel wept for Moses in the plains of Moab thirty days; so the days of weeping in the mourning for Moses were ended. And Joshua, the son of Nun, was full of the spirit of wisdom; for Moses had laid his hands upon him; and the children of Israel hearkened to him, and did as God commanded Moses. And there has not arisen a prophet since in Israel likened to Moses, whom God knew face-to-face; in all the signs and the wonders, which God sent him to do in the land of Egypt, to Pharaoh, and to all his servants, and to all his land; and in all the Mighty Hand, and in all the great awe, which Moses performed in the sight of all Israel."

The verses in this portion begin with the death of Moses and go on to describe where Moses was buried, the process of mourning him, and the leadership of Joshua, who replaced Moses as leader and prophet. The big question is: Who wrote these last verses? We know that Moses wrote the entire Torah, as revealed to him by the Creator, but who wrote the final eight verses after Moses died? Rabbi Yehuda says Joshua wrote them, but Rav Shimon bar Yochai says that's not possible. According to Rav Shimon, even the last eight verses were written by Moses. The difference, Rav Shimon says, between the rest of the Torah and these last eight verses is that earlier the Creator spoke and Moses wrote His words. But in the last eight verses, God spoke and Moses wrote *bedama*, "with tears." Still, this is very difficult to understand. What does it mean that Moses wrote "with tears"? How can a person write about his own death and the events immediately following when he is still alive? How could he know about them?

The kabbalists say that there is a difference between the prophecy of Moses and the prophecy of all the other prophets that ever lived. Most prophets were literally conduits for the words of the Creator. At the moment that they were giving voice to the Creator's prophecy, they did not even know what they were saying. Moses, though, was different. Even during his prophecies, Moses understood what he was saying and remembered it afterwards. This was true for all of the prophecy of Moses—except these last eight verses. In these verses, Moses was like the other prophets in that he was simply a conduit for the Creator. This was how Moses was able to write the words: "There died Moses, the servant of God. He was buried in this place." The words were being spoken by Moses, but not chosen by him.

There is another way of understanding this. The kabbalists tell us that the Torah is code, in the sense that we cannot accept its stories as literal when we read them. As a matter of fact, the *Zohar* tells us, if we accept the literal meaning of the Torah, we're missing the entire point. The power and the importance of the Torah lie not in its record of historical events, but in the deeper understanding that comes with study of the *Zohar* and of Kabbalah. Every letter, every verse in the Torah, has a deeper meaning. This is the Torah that existed two thousand years before the creation of our world, the Torah that is decoded by spiritual giants. Therefore, the kabbalists explain that when Moses revealed the Torah, he understood it on all levels. He was aware of the story he was recounting, but more importantly, he was able to access, in real time, its embedded meaning. So when Moses was revealing the story of his death, he was delivering the Light that lies beyond our understanding.

In this way, Moses is giving us a vitally important message in these last eight verses: Never accept the Torah, your life, or the world at face value. When you see things literally, they will seem sad or disappointing, but if you can push yourself to find the deeper meanings, to understand the hidden secrets, you arrive at a consciousness where there is no death, there is no sadness, and there is no pain. This is the second way to understand these last eight verses of the Torah.

There is yet another way to consider these last eight verses. The kabbalists tell us that there are actually four levels of the Torah, in keeping with the Four Worlds: *Atzilut* (Emanation), *Briah* (Creation), *Yetzirah* (Formation), and *Asiyah* (Action). The Torah that we know, the Bible that we read is coded according to the lowest world, the World of Action. In the World of *Atzilut*, for instance, the letters and words of the Torah and the letters do not appear in the same order as they do in ours. In the World of *Atzilut*, the place from which the essence of the Torah is actually revealed, all the many thousands of words, sentences, and paragraphs in the Torah actually exist as one name, formed in such a way that if a person were able to access it, he could create any miracle, reveal any Light.

The underlying code of the Torah is actually one name that takes the letters in our Torah and distills them into their purest, truest form. As the Torah descends into the lower worlds—from *Atzilut* to *Briah*, and from *Briah* to *Yetzirah*—it takes on a more material appearance. The kabbalists say that in the World of *Yetzirah*, for instance, letters combine to create the names of angels, since that is the world in which they exist. Only when the Torah comes into our physical world does it take on the words we see. So in this third interpretation, Moses wrote the last eight verses in the code of their source world, *Atzilut*. When Moses did so, he was connecting to the absolute essence of the Torah from a world where he was no longer bound by the existence of death.

As Moses leaves this world, he gives us the most important revelation of all: Don't just study; don't just understand; don't just do the spiritual work. Make it your goal to access the Torah of *Atzilut*, the teachings that take us to the home of immortality. And when you are able to read those words, you can do anything.

Kabbalah Centre Books

72 Names of God, The: Technology for the Soul
72 Names of God for Kids, The: A Treasury of Timeless Wisdom
72 Names of God Meditation Book, The
And You Shall Choose Life: An Essay on Kabbalah, the Purpose of Life, and Our True Spiritual Work
AstrologiK: Kabbalistic Astrology Guide for Children
Becoming Like God: Kabbalah and Our Ultimate Destiny
Beloved of My Soul: Letters of Our Master and Teacher Rav Yehuda Tzvi Brandwein to His Beloved Student, Kabbalist Rav Berg
Consciousness and the Cosmos (Previously Star Connection)
Days of Connection: A Guide to Kabbalah's Holidays and New Moons
Days of Power Part 1
Days of Power Part 2
Education of a Kabbalist
Energy of the Hebrew Letters, The
Fear is Not an Option
Finding the Light Through the Darkness: Inspirational Lessons Rooted in the Bible and the Zohar
God Wears Lipstick: Kabbalah for Women
Holy Grail, The: A Manifesto on the Zohar
If You Don't Like Your Life, Change It!: Using Kabbalah to Rewrite the Movie of Your Life
Immortality: The Inevitability of Eternal Life
Kabbalah Connection, The: Preparing the Soul for Pesach
Kabbalah for the Layman
Kabbalah Method, The: The Bridge Between Science and the Soul, Physics and Fulfillment, Quantum and the Creator
Kabbalah: The Power To Change Everything
Kabbalistic Astrology: And the Meaning of Our Lives
Kabbalistic Bible: Genesis
Kabbalistic Bible: Exodus
Kabbalistic Bible: Leviticus
Kabbalistic Bible: Numbers
Kabbalistic Bible: Deuteronomy

Light of Wisdom: On Wisdom, Life, and Eternity
Miracles, Mysteries, and Prayer Volume 1
Miracles, Mysteries, and Prayer Volume 2
Nano: Technology of Mind Over Matter
Navigating The Universe: A Roadmap for Understanding the Cosmic Influences that Shape Our Lives (Previously Time Zones)
On World Peace: Two Essays by the Holy Kabbalist Rav Yehuda Ashlag
Path to the Light: Decoding the Bible with Kabbalah: Book of Beresheet Volume 1
Path to the Light: Decoding the Bible with Kabbalah: Book of Beresheet Volume 2
Path to the Light: Decoding the Bible with Kabbalah: Book of Beresheet Volume 3
Path to the Light: Decoding the Bible with Kabbalah: Book of Beresheet Volume 4
Path to the Light: Decoding the Bible with Kabbalah: Book of Shemot Volume 5
Path to the Light: Decoding the Bible with Kabbalah: Book of Shemot Volume 6
Path to the Light: Decoding the Bible with Kabbalah: Book of Vayikra Volume 7
Path to the Light: Decoding the Bible with Kabbalah: Book of Bamdibar Volume 8
Path to the Light: Decoding the Bible with Kabbalah: Book of Bamdibar Volume 9
Power of Kabbalah, The: 13 Principles to Overcome Challenges and Achieve Fulfillment
Rethink Love: 3 Steps to Being the One, Attracting the One, and Becoming One
Satan: An Autobiography
Secret, The: Unlocking the Source of Joy & Fulfillment
Secrets of the Bible: Teachings from Kabbalistic Masters
Secrets of The Zohar: Stories and Meditations to Awaken the Heart
Simple Light: Wisdom from a Woman's Heart
Shabbat Connections
Taming Chaos: Harnessing the Secret Codes of the Universe to Make Sense of Our Lives

Thought of Creation, The: On the Individual, Humanity, and Their Ultimate Perfection
To Be Continued: Reincarnation & the Purpose of Our Lives
To the Power of One
True Prosperity: How to Have Everything
Two Unlikely People to Change the World: A Memoir by Karen Berg
Vokabbalahry: Words of Wisdom for Kids to Live By
Way of the Kabbalist, The: A User's Guide To Technology for the Soul
Well of Life: Kabbalistic Wisdom from a Depth of Knowledge
Wheels of the Soul: Kabbalah and Reincarnation
Wisdom of Truth, The: 12 Essays by the Holy Kabbalist Rav Yehuda Ashlag
Zohar, The

About the Zohar

The Zohar, the basic source of the Kabbalah, was authored two thousand years ago by Rabbi Shimon bar Yochai while hiding from the Romans in a cave in Peki'in for 13 years. It was later brought to light by Rabbi Moses de Leon in Spain, and further revealed through the Safed Kabbalists and the Lurianic system of Kabbalah.

The programs of The Kabbalah Centre have been established to provide opportunities for learning, teaching, research, and demonstration of specialized knowledge drawn from the ageless wisdom of the Zohar and the Jewish sages. Long kept from the masses, today this knowledge of the Zohar and Kabbalah should be shared by all who seek to understand the deeper meaning of this spiritual heritage, and a deeper and more profound meaning of life. Modern science is only beginning to discover what our sages veiled in symbolism. This knowledge is of a very practical nature and can be applied daily for the betterment of our lives and of humankind.

Darkness cannot prevail in the presence of Light. Even a darkened room must respond to the lighting of a candle. As we share this moment together we are beginning to witness, and indeed some of us are already participating in, a people's revolution of enlightenment. The darkened clouds of strife and conflict will make their presence felt only as long as the Eternal Light remains concealed.

The Zohar now remains an instrument to infuse the cosmos with the revealed Lightforce of the Creator. The Zohar is not a book about religion. Rather, the Zohar is concerned with the relationship between the unseen forces of the cosmos, the Lightforce, and the impact on humanity.

The Zohar promises that with the ushering in of the Age of Aquarius, the cosmos will become readily accessible to human understanding. It states that in the days of the Messiah "there will no longer be the necessity for one to request of his neighbor, teach me wisdom." (Zohar, Naso 9:65) "One day, they will no longer teach every man his neighbor and every man his brother, saying know the Lord. For they shall all know Me, from the youngest to the oldest of them. (Jeremiah 31:34) We can regain dominion of our lives and environment. To achieve this objective, the Zohar provides us with an opportunity to transcend the crushing weight of universal negativity.

The daily perusing of the Zohar, without any attempt at translation or understanding will fill our consciousness with the Light, improving our well-being, and influencing all in our environment toward positive attitudes. Even the scanning of the Zohar by those unfamiliar with the Hebrew Alef Bet will accomplish the same result.

The connection that we establish through scanning the Zohar is one of unity with the Light of the Creator. The letters, even if we do not consciously know Hebrew or Aramaic, are the channels through which the connection is made and can be likened to dialing a telephone number or typing in the codes to run a computer program. The connection is established at the metaphysical level of our being and radiates into our physical plane of existence. But first there is the prerequisite of metaphysical "fixing." We have to consciously, through positive thought and actions, permit the immense power of the Zohar to radiate love, harmony, and peace into our lives for us to share with all humanity and the universe.

As we enter the years ahead, the Zohar will continue to be a people's book, striking a sympathetic chord in the hearts and minds of those who long for peace, truth, and relief from suffering. In the face of crises and catastrophe, the Zohar has the ability to resolve agonizing human afflictions by restoring each individual's relationship with the Lightforce of the Creator.

—Rav Berg, 1984

About the Centres

Below is a statement written by Rav Berg in 1984. It remains true today.

Through the ultimate knowledge and mystical practices of Kabbalah, one can reach the highest spiritual levels attainable. Although many people rely on belief, faith, and dogmas in pursuing the meaning of life, Kabbalists seek a spiritual connection with the Creator and the forces of the Creator, so that the strange becomes familiar, and faith becomes knowledge.

Throughout history, those who knew and practiced the Kabbalah were extremely careful in their dissemination of the knowledge because they knew the masses of mankind had not yet prepared for the ultimate truth of existence. Today, kabbalists know that it is not only proper but necessary to make the Kabbalah available to all who seek it.

The Kabbalah Centre is an independent, non-profit institute founded in Israel in 1922. The Centre provides research, information, and assistance to those who seek the insights of Kabbalah. The Centre offers public lectures, classes, seminars, and excursions to mystical sites at branches in Israel and in the United States. Branches have been opened in Mexico, Montreal, Toronto, Paris, Hong Kong, and Taiwan.

Our courses and materials deal with the Zoharic understanding of each weekly portion of the Torah. Every facet of life is covered and other dimensions, hithertofore unknown, provide a deeper connection to a superior reality. Three important beginner courses cover such aspects as: Time, Space and Motion; Reincarnation, Marriage, Divorce; Kabbalistic Meditation; Limitation of the Five Senses; Illusion-Reality; Four Phases; Male and Female, Death, Sleep, Dreams; Food; and Shabbat.

Thousands of people have benefited from the Centre's activities, and the Centre's publishing of kabbalistic material continues to be the most comprehensive of its kind in the world, including translations in English, Hebrew, Russian, German, Portuguese, French, Spanish, Farsi (Persian).

Kabbalah can provide one with the true meaning of their being and the knowledge necessary for their ultimate benefit. It can show one spirituality that is beyond belief. The Kabbalah Centre will continue to make available the Kabbalah to all those who seek it.

—Rav Berg, 1984